Amish
COOKING

Publications International, Ltd.

All recipes and photographs that contain specific brand names are copyrighted by those companies and/or associations, unless otherwise specified. All photographs *except* those on pages 69, 103 and 123 copyright © Publications International, Ltd.

DOLE® is a registered trademark of Dole Food Company, Inc.

Carnation, Libby's, Nestlé and Toll House are registered trademarks of Nestlé.

SUNKIST is a registered trademark of Sunkist Growers, Inc.

Some of the products listed in this publication may be in limited distribution.

Pictured on the front cover: It's a Keeper Casserole *(page 51).*
Pictured on the back cover *(top to bottom):* Ground Beef, Spinach and Barley Soup *(page 70)* and Pumpkin Carrot Cake *(page 114).*

Front cover illustration by Robert Crawford.
Interior illustrations by Roberta Polfus.

ISBN-13: 978-1-60553-863-1
ISBN-10: 1-60553-863-9

Manufactured in China.

8 7 6 5 4 3 2 1

Microwave Cooking: Microwave ovens vary in wattage. Use the cooking times as guidelines and check for doneness before adding more time.

Preparation/Cooking Times: Preparation times are based on the approximate amount of time required to assemble the recipe before cooking, baking, chilling or serving. These times include preparation steps such as measuring, chopping and mixing. The fact that some preparations and cooking can be done simultaneously is taken into account. Preparation of optional ingredients and serving suggestions is not included.

Publications International, Ltd.

Contents

Meat and Poultry

Herbed Chicken & Vegetables

  2 **medium all-purpose potatoes, thinly sliced
     (about 1 pound)**
  2 **medium carrots, sliced**
  4 **bone-in chicken pieces (about 2 pounds)**
  1 **envelope LIPTON® RECIPE SECRETS® Savory
     Herb with Garlic Soup Mix**
 ⅓ **cup water**
  1 **tablespoon BERTOLLI® Olive Oil**

1. *Preheat oven to 425°F. In broiler pan without the rack, place potatoes and carrots; arrange chicken on top. Pour soup mix blended with water and oil over chicken and vegetables.*

2. *Bake uncovered 40 minutes or until chicken is thoroughly cooked, juices run clear and vegetables are tender.*   *Makes 4 servings*

Prep Time: *10 minutes*
Cook Time: *40 minutes*

Herbed Chicken & Vegetables

Roasted Turkey Breast with Cherry & Apple Rice Stuffing

3³/₄ cups water
3 boxes UNCLE BEN'S® Long Grain & Wild Rice
    Butter & Herb Fast Cook Recipe
¹/₂ cup butter or margarine, divided
¹/₂ cup dried red tart cherries
1 large apple, peeled and chopped (about 1 cup)
¹/₂ cup sliced almonds, toasted*
1 bone-in turkey breast (5 to 6 pounds)

*To toast almonds, place them on a baking sheet. Bake 10 to 12 minutes in a preheated 325°F oven or until they are golden brown, stirring occasionally.

1. In large saucepan, combine water, rice, contents of seasoning packets, 3 tablespoons butter and cherries. Bring to a boil. Cover; reduce heat to low and simmer 25 minutes or until all water is absorbed. Stir in apple and almonds; set aside.

2. Preheat oven to 325°F. Place turkey breast, skin side down, on rack in roasting pan. Loosely fill breast cavity with rice stuffing. Place any remaining stuffing in greased baking dish. Bake alongside turkey for 35 to 40 minutes or until heated through.

3. Place sheet of heavy-duty foil over stuffing, molding it slightly over sides of turkey. Carefully invert turkey, skin side up, on rack. Melt remaining 5 tablespoons butter; brush some of butter over surface of turkey.

4. Roast turkey, uncovered, 1 hour; baste with melted butter. Continue roasting 1 to 2 hours, basting occasionally with melted butter until meat thermometer inserted into center of thickest part of turkey breast, not touching bone, registers 170°F. Let turkey stand, covered, 15 minutes before carving.   *Makes 6 to 8 servings*

Roasted Turkey Breast with Cherry & Apple Rice Stuffing

Buttermilk Oven-Fried Chicken

1½ **cups buttermilk**
4 **teaspoons garlic powder, divided**
2 **teaspoons salt**
2 **teaspoons dried thyme, divided**
1 **teaspoon dried sage**
1 **teaspoon paprika**
½ **teaspoon black pepper**
2½ **pounds chicken pieces, skin removed**
   Nonstick cooking spray
1½ **cups dry bread crumbs**
¼ **cup all-purpose flour**

1. Whisk buttermilk, 3 teaspoons garlic powder, salt, 1 teaspoon thyme, sage, paprika and pepper in large bowl until well blended. Add chicken; turn to coat. Cover and refrigerate at least 5 hours or overnight.

2. Preheat oven to 400°F. Line two baking sheets with foil; spray with cooking spray.

3. Combine bread crumbs, flour, remaining 1 teaspoon garlic powder and 1 teaspoon thyme in large shallow bowl. Remove chicken from buttermilk mixture, allowing excess to drip off. Coat chicken pieces, one at a time, with crumb mixture. Shake off excess crumbs. Place on prepared baking sheets; let stand 10 minutes.

4. Bake about 50 minutes or until chicken is golden brown and juices run clear, turning once.   *Makes about 8 servings*

Buttermilk Oven-Fried Chicken

Chili Meatloaf and Potato Bake

1¹/₂ pounds ground turkey
³/₄ cup salsa
1 tablespoon chili powder
1 egg, beaten
1¹/₃ cups French's® French Fried Onions, divided
¹/₂ teaspoon salt
¹/₄ teaspoon ground black pepper
2 cups prepared hot mashed potatoes
2 cups (8 ounces) shredded taco blend cheese, divided

1. *Preheat oven to 375°F. Combine ground turkey, salsa, chili powder, egg, ²/₃ cup French Fried Onions, salt and pepper until blended. Press turkey mixture into 9-inch square baking dish.*

2. *Bake 25 minutes or until turkey is cooked through and juices run clear. Drain off fat.*

3. *Combine potatoes and 1 cup cheese. Spread evenly over meatloaf. Sprinkle with remaining cheese and onions; bake 5 minutes or until cheese is melted and onions are golden.*   *Makes 6 servings*

Prep Time: *15 minutes*
Cook Time: *30 minutes*

Tip: Prepare instant mashed potatoes for 4 servings.

*Variation: For added Cheddar flavor, substitute **French's®** Cheddar French Fried Onions for the original flavor.*

Chili Meatloaf and Potato Bake

Maple-Mustard Pork Chops

2 tablespoons maple syrup, divided
1 tablespoon olive oil
2 teaspoons whole-grain mustard
2 center-cut pork loin chops (6 ounces each)
  Nonstick cooking spray
$1/3$ cup water

1. *Preheat oven to 375°F. Combine maple syrup, olive oil and mustard in small bowl. Brush syrup mixture over both sides of pork chops.*

2. *Spray medium ovenproof skillet with cooking spray; heat skillet over medium-high heat. Add chops; brown on both sides. Add water; cover and bake 20 to 30 minutes or until barely pink in centers.*

Makes 2 servings

Kielbasa and Sauerkraut Skillet Dinner

2 tablespoons olive oil
1 pound kielbasa sausage, cut in $1/4$-inch-thick
  slices
1 red onion, thinly sliced
1 green bell pepper, cored, seeded and thinly sliced
2 cups sauerkraut, rinsed and well drained
2 teaspoons Dijon mustard
$1/2$ teaspoon caraway seeds
$1/4$ teaspoon salt
$1/4$ teaspoon black pepper

1. *Heat oil in large skillet. Add kielbasa, onion and bell pepper. Cook over medium heat 5 to 10 minutes or until vegetables are tender and sausage is lightly browned, stirring occasionally. Drain fat.*

2. *Add sauerkraut, mustard, caraway seeds, salt and black pepper to skillet. Cook over medium heat 3 to 5 minutes or until heated through.*

Makes 4 servings

Maple-Mustard Pork Chop

Roast Chicken with Peppers

1 cut-up whole chicken (3 to 3½ pounds)
3 tablespoons olive oil, divided
1 tablespoon plus 1½ teaspoons chopped fresh
   rosemary or 1½ teaspoons dried rosemary
1 tablespoon fresh lemon juice
1¼ teaspoons salt, divided
¾ teaspoon ground black pepper, divided
3 bell peppers (1 red, 1 yellow and 1 green)
1 onion
   Rosemary sprigs (optional)

1. Preheat oven to 375°F. Rinse chicken in cold water; pat dry with paper towels. Place in shallow roasting pan.

2. Combine 2 tablespoons oil, rosemary and lemon juice; brush over chicken. Sprinkle 1 teaspoon salt and ½ teaspoon pepper over chicken. Roast 15 minutes.

3. Cut bell peppers lengthwise into ½-inch-thick strips. Cut onion into thin wedges. Toss vegetables with remaining 1 tablespoon oil, ¼ teaspoon salt and ¼ teaspoon pepper. Spoon vegetables around chicken; roast about 40 minutes or until vegetables are tender and chicken is no longer pink. Serve chicken with vegetables and pan juices. Garnish with rosemary sprigs.   *Makes 6 servings*

Roast Chicken with Peppers

Country Chicken Stew with Dumplings

> 1 tablespoon BERTOLLI® Olive Oil
> 1 chicken (3 to 3¹/₂ pounds), cut into serving pieces
>   (with or without skin)
> 4 large carrots, cut into 2-inch pieces
> 3 ribs celery, cut into 1-inch pieces
> 1 large onion, cut into 1-inch wedges
> 1 envelope LIPTON® RECIPE SECRETS® Savory
>   Herb with Garlic Soup Mix*
> 1¹/₂ cups water
> ¹/₂ cup apple juice
>   Parsley Dumplings (recipe follows)

Also terrific with LIPTON® RECIPE SECRETS® Golden Onion Soup Mix.

In 6-quart Dutch oven or heavy saucepot, heat oil over medium-high heat and brown ¹/₂ of the chicken; remove and set aside. Repeat with remaining chicken. Return chicken to Dutch oven. Stir in carrots, celery, onion and soup mix blended with water and apple juice. Bring to a boil over high heat. Reduce heat to low; simmer covered 25 minutes or until chicken is thoroughly cooked, juices run clear and vegetables are tender.

Meanwhile, prepare Parsley Dumplings. Drop 12 rounded tablespoonfuls of batter into simmering broth around chicken. Continue simmering covered 10 minutes or until toothpick inserted into center of dumplings comes out clean. Season stew, if desired, with salt and pepper.   *Makes about 6 servings*

Parsley Dumplings: *In medium bowl, combine 1¹/₃ cups all-purpose flour, 2 teaspoons baking powder, 1 tablespoon chopped fresh parsley and ¹/₂ teaspoon salt; set aside. In measuring cup, blend ²/₃ cup milk, 2 tablespoons melted butter and 1 egg. Stir milk mixture into flour mixture just until blended.*

Variation: *Add 1 pound quartered red potatoes to stew with carrots; eliminate dumplings.*

Country Chicken Stew with Dumplings

Family-Style Creamy Chicken and Noodles

8 ounces uncooked yolk-free wide egg noodles
4 cups water
1 pound boneless skinless chicken breasts
1½ cups chopped onions
¾ cup chopped celery
½ teaspoon salt
½ teaspoon dried thyme
1 bay leaf
⅛ teaspoon white pepper
1 can (10 ounces) condensed cream of chicken soup, undiluted
½ cup nonfat buttermilk
Chopped parsley (optional)

1. Cook noodles according to package directions, omitting salt. Drain; set aside.

2. Meanwhile, bring water to a boil in Dutch oven over high heat. Add chicken breasts, onions, celery, salt, thyme, bay leaf and pepper. Return to a boil. Reduce heat to low; simmer uncovered, 35 minutes.

3. Remove chicken. Cut into ½-inch pieces; set aside. Increase heat to high. Return liquid in Dutch oven to a boil. Continue cooking until liquid and vegetables have reduced to 1 cup.

4. Remove from heat; discard bay leaf. Whisk in soup and buttermilk until well blended. Add chicken pieces and noodles; toss to blend. Sprinkle with parsley.   *Makes 4 servings*

Family-Style Creamy Chicken and Noodles

Wild Rice Meatball Primavera

   1 **pound ground turkey**
   $^1/_2$ **cup seasoned bread crumbs**
   1 **egg, beaten**
   2 **tablespoons oil**
   1 **can (10$^3/_4$ ounces) condensed cream of mushroom soup, undiluted**
   2 **cups water**
   1 **package (16 ounces) frozen broccoli medley, thawed**
   1 **box UNCLE BEN'S® Long Grain & Wild Rice Fast Cook Recipe**

1. *Combine turkey, bread crumbs and egg; mix well. Shape into 1$^1/_4$- to 1$^1/_2$-inch meatballs (about 20 to 22 meatballs).*

2. *Heat oil in large skillet over medium-high heat until hot. Cook meatballs 6 to 7 minutes or until brown on all sides. Drain on paper towels.*

3. *Combine soup and water in skillet; bring to a boil. Add meatballs, vegetables and contents of seasoning packet, reserving rice. Cover; reduce heat and simmer 5 minutes, stirring occasionally.*

4. *Add reserved rice to skillet; mix well. Cover; cook 5 minutes more or until hot. Remove from heat; stir well. Cover and let stand 5 minutes before serving.*   *Makes 6 servings*

Wild Rice Meatball Primavera

Baked Barbecue Chicken

1 cut-up whole chicken (3 pounds)
1 onion, cut into slices
1½ cups ketchup
½ cup packed light brown sugar
¼ cup Worcestershire sauce
2 tablespoons lemon juice
1 tablespoon liquid smoke (optional)

1. Preheat oven to 375°F. Spray 13×9-inch baking dish with nonstick cooking spray. Place chicken in prepared dish; top with onion.

2. Combine ketchup, brown sugar, Worcestershire, lemon juice and liquid smoke, if desired, in small saucepan. Heat over medium heat 2 to 3 minutes or until sugar dissolves. Pour over chicken.

3. Bake 1 hour or until juices run clear. Discard onion slices. Let stand 10 minutes before serving.   *Makes 6 servings*

Tip: Liquid smoke is a commercial product produced by infusing a liquid with smoke. Brush it on broiled meat or poultry to give it a grilled flavor or add it to marinades.

Baked Barbecue Chicken

Italian-Style Brisket

1 cup beef broth, divided
$^1/_2$ cup chopped onion
1 clove garlic, minced
1 can (about 14 ounces) diced tomatoes
$^3/_4$ teaspoon dried oregano
$^1/_4$ teaspoon dried thyme
$^1/_4$ teaspoon black pepper
1 beef brisket (about 1$^1/_4$ pounds)
3 cups sliced mushrooms
3 cups halved and thinly sliced zucchini
    (about 1 pound)
3 cups cooked egg noodles

1. Heat $^1/_4$ cup beef broth in Dutch oven. Add onion and garlic; cover and simmer 5 minutes.

2. Stir in tomatoes, remaining $^3/_4$ cup beef broth, oregano, thyme and pepper. Bring to a boil. Reduce heat to low; add beef brisket. Cover and simmer 1$^1/_2$ hours, basting occasionally with tomato mixture.

3. Add mushrooms and zucchini; simmer covered, 30 to 45 minutes or until beef is tender.

4. Remove beef. Simmer vegetable mixture 5 to 10 minutes to thicken slightly. Cut beef across the grain into thin slices. Serve beef with vegetable sauce and noodles. *Makes 6 servings*

Italian-Style Brisket

Home-Style Skillet Chicken

1 tablespoon Cajun seasoning blend
$\frac{1}{2}$ teaspoon plus $\frac{1}{8}$ teaspoon black pepper, divided
$\frac{1}{2}$ teaspoon salt, divided
4 chicken thighs
2 tablespoons vegetable oil
4 cloves garlic, minced
$\frac{3}{4}$ pound red or new potatoes (about 8), quartered
12 pearl onions, peeled*
1 cup baby carrots
2 ribs celery, halved lengthwise and sliced
   diagonally into $\frac{1}{2}$-inch pieces
$\frac{1}{2}$ red bell pepper, diced
2 tablespoons all-purpose flour
$1\frac{1}{2}$ cups canned chicken broth
2 tablespoons finely chopped fresh parsley

*To peel pearl onions, drop in boiling water for 30 seconds and plunge immediately into ice water. The peel should slide right off.

1. Combine Cajun seasoning, $\frac{1}{2}$ teaspoon pepper and $\frac{1}{4}$ teaspoon salt in small bowl. Rub mixture on all sides of chicken.

2. Heat oil in large heavy skillet over medium-high heat. Add garlic and chicken; cook until chicken is browned, about 3 minutes per side. Transfer chicken to plate; set aside.

3. Add potatoes, onions, carrots, celery and bell pepper to skillet. Cook and stir 3 minutes. Sprinkle flour over vegetables, stir to coat. Slowly stir in chicken broth, scraping up browned bits from bottom of skillet. Bring mixture to a boil, stirring constantly.

4. Reduce heat to medium-low. Return chicken to skillet. Cover and cook about 30 minutes or until cooked through (165°F). Increase heat to medium-high; cook, uncovered, about 5 minutes or until sauce is thickened. Season with remaining $\frac{1}{8}$ teaspoon pepper and $\frac{1}{4}$ teaspoon salt. Sprinkle with parsley before serving.   *Makes 4 servings*

Home-Style Skillet Chicken

Ham with Apple Cherry Sauce

1 (3-pound) canned ham
³/₄ cup apple juice, divided
2 tablespoons cornstarch
1 cup chopped apples
¹/₂ cup cherry or currant jelly

1. *Bake ham according to package directions.*

2. *Combine ¹/₄ cup apple juice and cornstarch in small bowl; stir until smooth. Set aside.*

3. *Place apples, jelly and remaining ¹/₂ cup apple juice in large saucepan; heat over medium-high heat. Cook 5 minutes. Add cornstarch mixture; cook and stir about 1 minute or until thickened.*

4. *Slice ham. Serve with sauce.*   *Makes 8 to 10 servings*

Ham with Apple Cherry Sauce

Quick & Easy Broccoli Chicken

1 (6.9-ounce) package RICE-A-RONI® Chicken
    Flavor
2 tablespoons butter or margarine
1 teaspoon dried basil
4 boneless, skinless chicken breast halves
    (about 1 pound)
2 cups broccoli flowerets
1 tomato, chopped
1 cup (4 ounces) shredded mozzarella or
    Cheddar cheese

1. In large skillet over medium heat, sauté rice-vermicelli mix with butter until vermicelli is golden brown.

2. Slowly stir in 2 cups water, basil and Special Seasonings. Bring to a boil. Place chicken over rice. Reduce heat to low. Cover; simmer 10 minutes.

3. Stir in broccoli and tomato. Cover; simmer 10 minutes or until rice is tender and chicken is no longer pink inside. Sprinkle with cheese. Cover; let stand 3 minutes or until cheese is melted.

Makes 4 servings

Prep Time: *5 minutes*
Cook Time: *30 minutes*

Variation: If you prefer, use green beans or whole-kernel corn instead of the broccoli.

Quick & Easy Broccoli Chicken

Casseroles

Pork with Savory Apple Stuffing

1 package (6 ounces) corn bread stuffing mix
1 can (14^1/$_2$ ounces) chicken broth
1 small apple, peeled, cored and chopped
^{1}/$_4$ cup chopped celery
1^1/$_3$ cups French's® French Fried Onions, divided
4 boneless pork chops, ^{3}/$_4$ inch thick
(about 1 pound)
^{1}/$_2$ cup peach-apricot sweet & sour sauce
1 tablespoon French's® Honey Dijon Mustard

1. Preheat oven to 375°F. Combine stuffing mix, broth, apple, celery and ^{2}/$_3$ cup French Fried Onions in large bowl. Spoon into bottom of greased shallow 2-quart baking dish. Arrange chops on top of stuffing.

2. Combine sweet & sour sauce with mustard in small bowl. Pour over pork. Bake 40 minutes or until pork is no longer pink in center.

3. Sprinkle with remaining onions. Bake 5 minutes or until onions are golden. *Makes 4 servings*

Prep Time: *10 minutes*
Cook Time: *45 minutes*

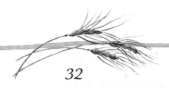

Pork with Savory Apple Stuffing

Chicken, Asparagus & Mushroom Bake

1 tablespoon butter
1 tablespoon olive oil
2 boneless skinless chicken breasts
    (about ½ pound), cut into bite-size pieces
2 cloves garlic, minced
1 cup sliced mushrooms
2 cups sliced asparagus
   Black pepper
1 package (about 6 ounces) corn bread
    stuffing mix
¼ cup dry white wine (optional)
1 can (about 14 ounces) chicken broth
1 can (10¾ ounces) condensed cream of asparagus
    or cream of chicken soup, undiluted

1. Preheat oven to 350°F. Heat butter and oil in large skillet until butter is melted. Cook and stir chicken and garlic about 3 minutes over medium-high heat until chicken is no longer pink. Add mushrooms; cook and stir 2 minutes. Add asparagus; cook and stir about 5 minutes or until asparagus is crisp-tender. Season with pepper.

2. Transfer mixture to 2½-quart casserole or 6 small casseroles. Top with stuffing mix.

3. Add wine to skillet, if desired; cook and stir 1 minute over medium-high heat, scraping up any browned bits from bottom of skillet. Add broth and soup; cook and stir until well blended.

4. Pour broth mixture into casserole; mix well. Bake uncovered, about 35 minutes (30 minutes for small casseroles) or until heated through and lightly browned.   *Makes 6 servings*

Chicken, Asparagus & Mushroom Bake

Potato Sausage Casserole

1 pound bulk pork sausage or ground pork
1 can (10 3/4 ounces) condensed cream of
    mushroom soup, undiluted
3/4 cup milk
1/2 cup chopped onion
1/2 teaspoon salt
1/4 teaspoon black pepper
3 cups sliced potatoes
1/2 tablespoon butter, cut into small pieces
1 1/2 cups (6 ounces) shredded Cheddar cheese
    Parsley (optional)

1. Preheat oven to 350°F. Spray 1 1/2-quart casserole with nonstick cooking spray. Brown sausage 6 to 8 minutes in large skillet over medium-high heat, stirring break up meat. Drain fat.

2. Combine soup, milk, onion, salt and pepper in medium bowl.

3. Place half of potatoes in prepared casserole. Top with half of soup mixture; top with half of sausage. Repeat layers. Dot with butter.

4. Cover pan with foil. Bake 1 1/4 to 1 1/2 hours or until potatoes are tender. Uncover; sprinkle with cheese. Return to oven; bake until cheese is melted and bubbly. Garnish with parsley.

Makes 6 servings

Potato Sausage Casserole

Spicy Chicken Casserole with Cornbread

2 tablespoons olive oil
4 boneless skinless chicken breasts, cut into
     bite-size pieces
1 envelope (about 1 ounce) taco seasoning
1 can (about 15 ounces) black beans, rinsed and
     drained
1 can (about 14 ounces) diced tomatoes, drained
1 can (about 10 ounces) Mexican-style corn,
     drained
1 can (about 4 ounces) diced chiles, drained
$\frac{1}{2}$ cup mild salsa
1 box (about 8 ounces) cornbread mix, plus
     ingredients to prepare mix
$\frac{1}{2}$ cup (2 ounces) shredded Cheddar cheese
$\frac{1}{4}$ cup chopped red bell pepper plus additional
     for garnish
     Parsley (optional)

1. Preheat oven to 350°F. Spray 2-quart casserole with nonstick cooking spray. Heat oil in large skillet over medium heat. Add chicken; cook and stir 5 minutes or until cooked through (165°F).

2. Sprinkle taco seasoning over chicken. Add black beans, tomatoes, corn, chiles and salsa; stir until well mixed. Transfer to prepared dish.

3. Prepare cornbread mix according to package directions, adding cheese and bell pepper. Spread batter over chicken mixture.

4. Bake 30 minutes or until corn bread is golden brown. Garnish with additional bell pepper and parsley.   *Makes 4 to 6 servings*

Spicy Chicken Casserole with Cornbread

Classic Macaroni and Cheese

2 cups elbow macaroni
3 tablespoons butter or margarine
$1/4$ cup chopped onion (optional)
2 tablespoons all-purpose flour
$1/2$ teaspoon salt
$1/8$ teaspoon pepper
2 cups milk
2 cups (8 ounces) SARGENTO® Chef Style or Fancy
 Mild Cheddar Shredded Cheese, divided

Cook macaroni according to package directions; drain. In medium saucepan, melt butter and, if desired, cook onion about 5 minutes or until tender. Stir in flour, salt and pepper. Gradually add milk and cook, stirring occasionally, until thickened. Remove from heat. Add $1^{1}/2$ cups cheese and stir until cheese melts. Combine cheese sauce with cooked macaroni. Place in $1^{1}/2$-quart casserole; top with remaining $1/2$ cup cheese. Bake at 350°F 30 minutes or until bubbly and cheese is golden brown.   *Makes 6 servings*

Tip: For a smooth cheese sauce, remove the sauce mixture from the heat and stir in the shredded cheese until it is completely melted.

Classic Macaroni and Cheese

Chicken Pot Pie with Onion Biscuits

1 package (1.8 ounces) classic white sauce mix
2³/₄ cups milk, divided
¹/₄ teaspoon dried thyme leaves
1 package (10 ounces) frozen peas and carrots, thawed
1 package (10 ounces) roasted carved chicken breast, cut into bite-size pieces
1 cup all-purpose baking mix
1¹/₃ cups French's® French Fried Onions, divided
¹/₂ cup (2 ounces) shredded Cheddar cheese

1. Preheat oven to 400°F. Prepare white sauce mix according to package directions with 2¹/₄ cups milk; stir in thyme. Mix vegetables, chicken and prepared white sauce in shallow 2-quart casserole.

2. Combine baking mix, ²/₃ cup French Fried Onions and remaining ¹/₂ cup milk in medium bowl until blended. Drop 6 to 8 spoonfuls of dough over chicken mixture.

3. Bake 25 minutes or until biscuits are golden. Sprinkle biscuits with cheese and remaining onions. Bake 3 minutes or until cheese is melted and onions are golden. *Makes 6 servings*

Prep Time: 15 minutes
Cook Time: 33 minutes

Tip: You may substitute 2 cups cut-up cooked chicken for the roasted, carved chicken breast.

Variation: For added Cheddar flavor, substitute **French's®** Cheddar French Fried Onions for the original flavor.

Chicken Pot Pie with Onion Biscuits

Beef Stroganoff Casserole

1 pound ground beef
1/4 teaspoon salt
1/8 teaspoon black pepper
1 teaspoon vegetable oil
8 ounces sliced mushrooms
1 onion, chopped
3 cloves garlic, minced
1/4 cup beef broth
1 can (10¾ ounces) condensed cream of mushroom
    soup, undiluted
1/2 cup sour cream
1 tablespoon Dijon mustard
4 cups cooked egg noodles
    Chopped fresh parsley (optional)
    Radish slices (optional)

1. Preheat oven to 350°F. Spray 13×9-inch baking dish with nonstick cooking spray.

2. Season beef with salt and pepper. Brown beef 6 to 8 minutes in large skillet over medium-high heat, stirring to break up meat. Drain fat. Remove beef to plate.

3. Heat oil in same skillet over medium-high heat. Add mushrooms, onion and garlic; cook and stir 2 minutes or until onion is tender. Add broth; reduce heat to medium-low and simmer 3 minutes. Remove from heat; stir in soup, sour cream and mustard until well blended. Return beef to skillet.

4. Place noodles in prepared dish. Pour beef mixture over noodles; stir until noodles are well coated. Bake uncovered, 30 minutes or until heated through. Sprinkle with parsley and radishes.

Makes 6 servings

Beef Stroganoff Casserole

Spicy Pork Chop Casserole

Nonstick cooking spray
2 cups frozen corn
2 cups frozen diced hash brown potatoes
1 can (about 14 ounces) diced tomatoes with basil, garlic, and oregano, drained
2 teaspoons chili powder
1 teaspoon dried oregano
$1/2$ teaspoon ground cumin
$1/8$ teaspoon crushed red pepper
1 teaspoon olive oil
4 (3-ounce) boneless pork loin chops, cut about $3/4$ inch thick
$1/4$ teaspoon black pepper
$1/4$ cup (1 ounce) shredded Monterey Jack cheese (optional)

1. Preheat oven to 375°F. Spray 8-inch square baking dish with cooking spray.

2. Spray large nonstick skillet with cooking spray. Add corn; cook and stir over medium-high heat about 5 minutes or until corn begins to brown. Add potatoes; cook and stir about 5 minutes or until potatoes begin to brown. Add tomatoes, chili powder, oregano, cumin and red pepper; stir until well blended. Transfer corn mixture to prepared dish.

3. Wipe skillet with paper towel. Add oil and pork chops to skillet. Cook pork chops over medium-high heat until brown on one side. Remove pork chops; place browned side up on top of corn mixture in baking dish. Sprinkle with pepper. Bake uncovered, 20 minutes or until barely pink in center. Sprinkle with cheese, if desired. Let stand 2 to 3 minutes.   *Makes 4 servings*

Prep Time: 15 minutes
Bake Time: 20 minutes

Spicy Pork Chop Casserole

Chicken Divan Casserole

1 cup uncooked rice
1 cup coarsely shredded carrots*
　Nonstick cooking spray
4 boneless skinless chicken breasts
1 pound frozen broccoli florets
2 tablespoons butter or margarine
3 tablespoons all-purpose flour
$1/4$ teaspoon salt
　Black pepper
1 cup chicken broth
$3/4$ cup milk or half-and-half
$1/3$ cup plus 2 tablespoons grated Parmesan cheese,
　divided

Coarsely shredded carrots are available in the produce sections of many large supermarkets or shred them on a hand-held grater.

1. Preheat oven to 350°F. Grease 12×8-inch baking dish.

2. Prepare rice according to package directions. Stir in carrots. Spread mixture into prepared baking dish.

3. Spray large skillet with cooking spray. Heat over medium-high heat. Brown chicken breasts about 2 minutes on each side. Arrange over rice. Arrange broccoli around chicken.

4. To prepare sauce, melt butter in 2-quart saucepan over medium heat. Whisk in flour, salt and pepper; cook and stir 1 minute. Gradually whisk in broth and milk. Cook and stir until mixture comes to a boil. Reduce heat; simmer 2 minutes. Remove from heat. Stir in $1/3$ cup cheese.

5. Pour sauce over chicken and broccoli. Sprinkle with remaining 2 tablespoons cheese. Cover with foil; bake 30 minutes. Remove foil; bake 10 to 15 minutes or until chicken is no longer pink in center.

Makes 6 servings

Chicken Divan Casserole

Oven-Baked Stew

2 pounds boneless beef chuck or round steak,
  cut into 1-inch cubes
¼ cup all-purpose flour
1⅓ cups sliced carrots
1 can (14 to 16 ounces) whole peeled tomatoes,
  undrained and chopped
1 envelope LIPTON® RECIPE SECRETS® Onion
  Soup Mix*
½ cup dry red wine or water
1 cup fresh or canned sliced mushrooms
1 package (8 ounces) medium or broad egg
  noodles, cooked and drained

Also terrific with LIPTON® RECIPE SECRETS® Beefy Onion, Onion Mushroom or Beefy Mushroom Soup Mix.

1. Preheat oven to 425°F. In 2½-quart shallow casserole, toss beef with flour, then bake uncovered 20 minutes, stirring once.

2. Reduce heat to 350°F. Stir in carrots, tomatoes, soup mix and wine.

3. Bake covered 1½ hours or until beef is tender. Stir in mushrooms and bake covered an additional 10 minutes. Serve over hot noodles.

Makes 8 servings

Prep Time: 20 minutes
Cook Time: 2 hours

It's a Keeper Casserole

1 tablespoon vegetable oil
$1/2$ cup chopped onion
$1/4$ cup chopped green bell pepper
1 clove garlic, minced
2 tablespoons all-purpose flour
1 teaspoon sugar
$1/2$ teaspoon each salt, dried basil and black pepper
1 package (about 16 ounces) frozen meatballs, cooked
1 can (about 14 ounces) whole tomatoes, cut up and drained
$1^{1}/2$ cups cooked vegetables (any combination)
1 teaspoon each beef bouillon granules and Worcestershire sauce
1 can refrigerated buttermilk biscuits

1. Preheat oven to 400°F. Heat oil in large saucepan over medium heat. Cook and stir onion, bell pepper and garlic until vegetables are tender.

2. Stir in flour, sugar, salt, basil and black pepper. Slowly blend in meatballs, tomatoes, vegetables, bouillon and Worcestershire. Cook and stir until slightly thickened and bubbly; pour into 2-quart casserole.

3. Unroll biscuits; place on top of casserole. Bake, uncovered, 15 minutes or until biscuits are golden.   *Makes 4 servings*

Soups and Salads

Cheddar Broccoli Soup

1 tablespoon olive oil
1 rib celery, chopped (about $^1/_2$ cup)
1 carrot, chopped (about $^1/_2$ cup)
1 small onion, chopped (about $^1/_2$ cup)
$^1/_2$ teaspoon dried thyme leaves, crushed (optional)
2 cans (13$^3/_4$ ounces each) chicken broth
1 jar (1 pound) RAGÚ® Cheese Creations!® Double
    Cheddar Sauce
1 box (10 ounces) frozen chopped broccoli, thawed
    and drained

In 3-quart saucepan, heat olive oil over medium heat and cook celery, carrot, onion and thyme 3 minutes or until vegetables are almost tender. Add chicken broth and bring to a boil over high heat. Reduce heat to medium and simmer, uncovered, 10 minutes.

In food processor or blender, purée vegetable mixture until smooth; return to saucepan. Stir in Ragú Cheese Creations! Double Cheddar Sauce and broccoli. Cook 10 minutes or until heated through.

Makes 6 (1-cup) servings

Cheddar Broccoli Soup

Country Chicken Chowder

1 pound chicken tenders, cut into $^1/_2$-inch pieces
2 tablespoons butter or margarine
1 onion, chopped
1 rib celery, sliced
1 carrot, sliced
1 can (10$^3/_4$ ounces) condensed cream
   of potato soup, undiluted
1 cup milk
1 cup frozen corn
$^1/_2$ teaspoon dried dill weed
   Salt and black pepper

1. Melt butter in large saucepan or Dutch oven over medium-high heat. Add chicken; cook and stir 5 minutes.

2. Add onion, celery and carrot; cook and stir 3 minutes. Stir in soup, milk, corn and dill; reduce heat to low. Cook about 8 minutes or until corn is tender and chowder is heated through. Season with salt and pepper.

Makes 4 servings

Prep and Cook Time: *27 minutes*

Tip: For a special touch, garnish soup with croutons and fresh dill. For a hearty winter meal, serve the chowder in hollowed-out toasted French rolls or small round sourdough loaves.

Country Chicken Chowder

Chunky Potato Bacon Soup

1 package (32 ounces) frozen Southern-style hash
  brown potatoes, thawed
1 quart milk
1 can (10¾ ounces) condensed cream of celery
  soup
1 cup (6 ounces) cubed processed cheese
⅓ cup cooked chopped bacon (4 slices uncooked)
1 tablespoon French's® Worcestershire Sauce
1⅓ cups French's® French Fried Onions

1. Combine potatoes, milk, soup, cheese, bacon and Worcestershire in large saucepot. Heat to boiling over medium-high heat, stirring often.

2. Heat French Fried Onions in microwave on HIGH 2 minutes or until golden. Ladle soup into bowls. Sprinkle with onions. Garnish with fresh minced parsley if desired.   *Makes 6 servings*

Prep Time: 5 minutes
Cook Time: 10 minutes

Tip: A good soup pot in one that is heavy and conducts and distributes heat evenly. Copper is the ideal metal, but good alternatives are aluminum and stainless steel.

Chunky Potato Bacon Soup

Country Bean Soup

1¼ cups dried navy beans or lima beans, rinsed and
   drained
2½ cups water, plus additional for boiling
  4 ounces salt pork or fully cooked ham, chopped
 ¼ cup chopped onion
 ½ teaspoon dried oregano
 ¼ teaspoon salt
 ¼ teaspoon ground ginger
 ¼ teaspoon dried sage
 ¼ teaspoon black pepper
  2 cups milk
  2 tablespoons butter

1. *Place navy beans in large saucepan; add enough water to cover. Bring to a boil; reduce heat and simmer 2 minutes. Remove from heat; cover and let stand for 1 hour. (Or cover beans with water and soak overnight.)*

2. *Drain beans and return to saucepan. Stir in 2½ cups water, pork, onion, oregano, salt, ginger, sage and pepper. Bring to a boil; reduce heat. Cover and simmer 2 to 2½ hours or until beans are tender. (If necessary, add more water during cooking.) Add milk and butter, stirring until mixture is heated through and butter is melted.*

Makes 6 servings

Country Bean Soup

Sensational Seven Layer Rice Salad

1 (7.2-ounce) package RICE-A-RONI® Rice Pilaf
2 tablespoons butter or margarine
1 (15-ounce) can black beans, drained and rinsed
1 cup ranch dressing
1 cup sour cream
4 cups fresh spinach leaves or romaine lettuce, cut into thin strips
3 medium tomatoes, chopped
2 cups (8 ounces) shredded Cheddar cheese
1 small red onion, halved and thinly sliced
$^1/_2$ pound bacon, crisply cooked, drained and chopped
3 radishes, sliced (optional)
Tomato wedges (optional)

1. In large skillet over medium heat, sauté rice-pasta mix with butter until pasta is golden brown.

2. Slowly add 1¾ cups water and Special Seasonings; bring to a boil. Reduce heat to low. Cover; simmer 17 to 22 minutes or until rice is tender.

3. Stir in black beans. Spread mixture in 13×9-inch baking pan. Cool completely; set aside.

4. In small bowl, mix ranch dressing and sour cream; set aside.

5. In large clear glass bowl, layer spinach, tomatoes, cheese, rice-bean mixture and onion, pressing gently after each layer. Spread dressing mixture over top of salad. Sprinkle with bacon. Garnish with radishes and tomato, if desired.   *Makes 8 servings*

Prep Time: *30 minutes*
Cook Time: *25 minutes*

Sensational Seven Layer Rice Salad

Pork and Cabbage Soup

½ pound pork loin, cut into ½-inch cubes
1 onion, chopped
2 strips bacon, finely chopped
1 can (about 28 ounces) tomatoes, cut-up and
    drained
2 cups canned beef broth
2 cups canned chicken broth
2 carrots, sliced
¾ teaspoon dried marjoram
1 bay leaf
⅛ teaspoon black pepper
¼ medium cabbage, chopped
2 tablespoons chopped fresh parsley, plus
    additional for garnish

1. Cook and stir pork, onion and bacon in 5-quart Dutch oven over medium heat until barely pink in center and onion is slightly tender. Drain fat.

2. Stir in tomatoes, broth, carrots, marjoram, bay leaf and pepper; bring to a boil over high heat. Reduce heat to medium-low; simmer uncovered, about 30 minutes. Remove and discard bay leaf. Skim off fat.

3. Stir cabbage into soup. Bring to a boil over high heat. Reduce heat to medium-low; simmer uncovered, about 15 minutes or until cabbage is tender.

4. Remove soup from heat; stir in 2 tablespoons parsley. Ladle into bowls. Garnish each serving with additional parsley.

Makes 6 servings

Pork and Cabbage Soup

Easy Chicken Salad

¼ cup finely diced celery
¼ cup mayonnaise
2 tablespoons sweet pickle relish
1 tablespoon minced onion
½ teaspoon Dijon mustard
⅛ teaspoon salt
Black pepper
2 cups cubed cooked chicken
Salad greens (optional)
Red grapes (optional)

1. Combine celery, mayonnaise, relish, onion, mustard, salt and pepper in medium bowl; mix well. Stir in chicken. Cover and refrigerate at least 1 hour.

2. Serve on salad greens with grapes, if desired.   *Makes 2 servings*

Inside-Out Egg Salad

6 hard-cooked eggs, peeled
⅓ cup mayonnaise
¼ cup chopped celery
1 tablespoon French's® Classic Yellow® Mustard

1. Cut eggs in half lengthwise. Remove egg yolks. Combine yolks, mayonnaise, celery and mustard in small bowl. Add salt and pepper to taste.

2. Spoon egg yolk mixture into egg whites. Sprinkle with paprika, if desired. Chill before serving.   *Makes 12 servings*

Prep Time: *20 minutes*

Easy Chicken Salad

Corn and Tomato Chowder

1½ **cups peeled, diced plum tomatoes**
¾ **teaspoon salt, divided**
2 **ears corn, husks removed**
1 **tablespoon butter**
½ **cup finely chopped shallots**
1 **clove garlic, minced**
1 **can (12 ounces) evaporated milk**
1 **cup chicken broth**
1 **tablespoon finely chopped fresh sage or**
   1 **teaspoon rubbed sage, plus additional**
   for garnish
¼ **teaspoon black pepper**
1 **tablespoon cornstarch**
2 **tablespoons cold water**

1. *Place tomatoes in nonmetal colander over bowl. Sprinkle with
½ teaspoon salt; toss to mix well. Allow tomatoes to drain at least
1 hour.*

2. *Meanwhile, cut corn kernels off cobs into small bowl. Scrape cobs
with dull side of knife blade to extract liquid from cobs into same
bowl; set aside. Discard 1 cob; break remaining cob in half.*

3. *Heat butter in heavy medium saucepan over medium-high heat
until melted and bubbly. Add shallots and garlic; reduce heat to
low. Cover and cook about 5 minutes or until shallots are soft and
translucent. Add evaporated milk, broth, sage, pepper and reserved
corn cob halves. Bring to a boil over high heat. Reduce heat to low;
simmer uncovered, 10 minutes. Remove and discard cob halves.*

4. *Add corn with liquid; return to a boil over medium-high heat.
Reduce heat to low; simmer uncovered, 15 minutes. Dissolve
cornstarch in water; stir into chowder until thickened. Remove from
heat; stir in drained tomatoes and remaining ¼ teaspoon salt.
Garnish with additional fresh sage, if desired.*   *Makes 4 servings*

Corn and Tomato Chowder

Tuna Pasta Primavera Salad

2 cups cooked and chilled small shell pasta
1½ cups halved cherry tomatoes
½ cup thinly sliced carrots
½ cup sliced celery
½ cup chopped seeded peeled cucumber
½ cup thinly sliced radishes
½ cup thawed frozen peas
¼ cup slivered red bell pepper
2 tablespoons minced green onion, including tops
1 (7-ounce) pouch of STARKIST® Premium Albacore
   or Chunk Light Tuna
1 cup salad dressing of choice
  Bibb or red leaf lettuce
  Fresh herbs, for garnish

In large bowl, combine all ingredients except lettuce and herbs. Chill several hours. If using oil and vinegar dressing, stir salad mixture occasionally to evenly marinate ingredients. Place lettuce leaves on each plate; spoon salad over lettuce. Garnish with fresh herbs, if desired.   *Makes 6 servings*

Prep Time: *25 minutes*

Tuna Pasta Primavera Salad

Ground Beef, Spinach and Barley Soup

    12 **ounces ground beef**
     4 **cups water**
     1 **can (about 14 ounces) stewed tomatoes**
   1½ **cups thinly sliced carrots**
     1 **cup chopped onion**
    ½ **cup quick-cooking barley**
   1½ **teaspoons beef bouillon granules**
   1½ **teaspoons dried thyme**
     1 **teaspoon dried oregano**
    ½ **teaspoon garlic powder**
    ¼ **teaspoon black pepper**
    ⅛ **teaspoon salt**
     3 **cups torn stemmed spinach leaves**

1. Brown beef 6 to 8 minutes in large saucepan over medium heat, stirring to break up meat. Drain fat. Add water, tomatoes, carrots, onion, barley, bouillon, thyme, oregano, garlic powder, pepper and salt.

2. Bring to a boil over high heat. Reduce heat to medium-low. Cover and simmer 12 to 15 minutes or until barley and vegetables are tender, stirring occasionally. Stir in spinach; cook until spinach starts to wilt.

Makes 4 servings

Tip: Fresh spinach leaves cook very quickly. Add them to this soup just before serving and cook for only a minute until they lose their crispness.

Ground Beef, Spinach and Barley Soup

Side Dishes

Savory Skillet Broccoli

1 tablespoon BERTOLLI® Olive Oil
6 cups fresh broccoli florets or 1 pound green
    beans, trimmed
1 envelope LIPTON® RECIPE SECRETS® Golden
    Onion Soup Mix*
1¹/₂ cups water

*Also terrific with LIPTON® RECIPE SECRETS® Onion Mushroom Soup Mix.

1. In 12-inch skillet, heat oil over medium-high heat and cook broccoli, stirring occasionally, 2 minutes.

2. Stir in soup mix blended with water. Bring to a boil over high heat.

3. Reduce heat to medium-low and simmer covered 6 minutes or until broccoli is tender.   Makes 4 servings

Prep Time: 5 minutes
Cook Time: 10 minutes

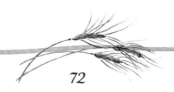

Savory Skillet Broccoli

Bacon and Maple Grits Puff

8 slices bacon
2 cups milk
1¼ cups water
1 cup quick-cooking grits
½ teaspoon salt
½ cup pure maple syrup
4 eggs
Fresh chives (optional)

1. Preheat oven to 350°F. Grease 1½-quart round casserole or soufflé dish; set aside.

2. Cook bacon in large skillet over medium-high heat about 7 minutes or until crisp. Remove bacon to paper towel; set aside. Reserve 2 tablespoons bacon drippings.

3. Combine milk, water, grits and salt in medium saucepan. Bring to a boil over medium heat, stirring frequently. Simmer 2 to 3 minutes or until mixture thickens, stirring constantly. Remove from heat; stir in syrup and reserved 2 tablespoons bacon drippings.

4. Crumble bacon; reserve ¼ cup for garnish. Stir remaining crumbled bacon into grits mixture.

5. Beat eggs in medium bowl. Gradually stir small amount of grits mixture into eggs, then stir back into remaining grits mixture. Pour into prepared casserole.

6. Bake 1 hour and 20 minutes or until knife inserted into center comes out clean. Top with reserved ¼ cup bacon. Garnish with chives. Serve immediately.   *Makes 6 to 8 servings*

Note: Puff will fall slightly after removing from oven.

Bacon and Maple Grits Puff

Festive Cranberry Mold

$^{1}/_{2}$ cup water
1 package (6 ounces) raspberry gelatin
1 can (8 ounces) cranberry sauce
1$^{2}/_{3}$ cups cranberry juice cocktail
1 cup sliced bananas (optional)
$^{1}/_{2}$ cup walnuts, toasted (optional)

1. Bring water to a boil in medium saucepan over medium-high heat. Add gelatin and stir until dissolved. Fold in cranberry sauce. Reduce heat to medium; cook until sauce is melted. Stir in cranberry juice cocktail.

2. Refrigerate mixture until slightly thickened. Fold in banana slices and walnuts, if desired. Pour mixture into 4-cup mold; cover and refrigerate until gelatin is set.   *Makes 8 servings*

Chunky Applesauce

10 tart apples (about 3 pounds) peeled,
      cored and chopped
$^{3}/_{4}$ cup packed light brown sugar
$^{1}/_{2}$ cup apple juice or apple cider
1$^{1}/_{2}$ teaspoons ground cinnamon
$^{1}/_{8}$ teaspoon salt
$^{1}/_{8}$ teaspoon ground nutmeg

1. Combine apples, brown sugar, apple juice, cinnamon, salt and nutmeg in heavy, large saucepan; cover. Cook over medium-low heat 40 to 45 minutes or until apples are tender, stirring occasionally. Remove saucepan from heat. Cool completely.

2. Store in airtight container in refrigerator up to 1 month.
                                     Makes about 5$^{1}/_{2}$ cups

Festive Cranberry Mold

Golden Corn Pudding

2 tablespoons butter or margarine
3 tablespoons all-purpose flour
1 can (14¾ ounces) DEL MONTE® Cream Style
    Golden Sweet Corn
¼ cup yellow cornmeal
2 eggs, separated
1 package (3 ounces) cream cheese, softened
1 can (8¾ ounces) DEL MONTE Whole Kernel
    Golden Sweet Corn, drained

1. Preheat oven to 350°F.

2. Melt butter in medium saucepan. Add flour and stir until smooth. Blend in cream style corn and cornmeal. Bring to a boil over medium heat, stirring constantly.

3. Place egg yolks in small bowl; stir in ½ cup hot mixture. Pour mixture back into saucepan. Add cream cheese and whole kernel corn.

4. Place egg whites in clean narrow bowl and beat until stiff peaks form. With rubber spatula, gently fold egg whites into corn mixture.

5. Pour mixture into 1½-quart straight-sided baking dish. Bake 30 to 35 minutes or until lightly browned.   *Makes 4 to 6 servings*

Prep Time: 10 minutes
Bake Time: 35 minutes

Tip: Pudding can be prepared up to 3 hours ahead of serving time. Cover and refrigerate until about 30 minutes before baking.

Asparagus with Dijon Mayonnaise

1 pound DOLE® Fresh Asparagus, trimmed
²/₃ cup fat-free or reduced-fat mayonnaise
2 tablespoons finely chopped DOLE® Green Onions
1 tablespoon lemon juice
1 tablespoon Dijon-style mustard
¹/₄ teaspoon prepared horseradish
   Parsley (optional)

• Cook asparagus in boiling water 3 to 5 minutes or until tender-crisp; drain. Rinse in cold water; drain.

• Stir together mayonnaise, green onions, lemon juice, mustard and horseradish in bowl until blended. Garnish with parsley, if desired. Serve asparagus with dip.   *Makes 6 servings*

Prep Time: 10 minutes
Cook Time: 5 minutes

Garlic Mayonnaise: Omit mustard; stir in 2 garlic cloves, finely chopped and 2 tablespoons finely chopped fresh parsley.

Herb Mayonnaise: Omit mustard; stir in 2 tablespoons nonfat milk and ¹/₂ teaspoon each dill weed, dried basil leaves and dried rosemary.

Zucchini Delight

1 can (10³/₄ ounces) condensed tomato soup,
   undiluted
1 tablespoon lemon juice
1 teaspoon sugar
2 cloves garlic, minced
¹/₂ teaspoon salt
6 cups (¹/₂-inch) zucchini slices
1 cup thinly sliced onion
1 cup coarsely chopped green bell pepper
1 cup sliced mushrooms
2 tablespoons grated Parmesan cheese

1. Combine soup, lemon juice, sugar, garlic and salt in large saucepan; mix well. Add zucchini, onion, bell pepper and mushrooms; mix well. Bring to a boil; reduce heat.

2. Cover and cook 20 to 25 minutes or until vegetables are crisp-tender, stirring occasionally. Sprinkle with cheese before serving.

Makes 6 servings

Tip: Zucchini are available throughout the year, but their peak season is from July to September.

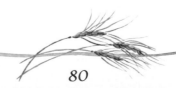

Zucchini Delight

Broccoli Casserole with Crumb Topping

2 slices day-old white bread, coarsely crumbled
   (about 1¼ cups)
½ cup shredded mozzarella cheese (about 2 ounces)
2 tablespoons chopped fresh parsley (optional)
2 tablespoons BERTOLLI® Olive Oil
1 clove garlic, finely chopped
6 cups broccoli florets and/or cauliflowerets
1 envelope LIPTON® RECIPE SECRETS® Onion
   Soup Mix
1 cup water
1 large tomato, chopped

1. In small bowl, combine bread crumbs, cheese, parsley, 1 tablespoon oil and garlic; set aside.

2. In 12-inch skillet, heat remaining 1 tablespoon oil over medium heat and cook broccoli, stirring frequently, 2 minutes.

3. Stir in onion soup mix blended with water. Bring to a boil over high heat. Reduce heat to low and simmer uncovered, stirring occasionally, 8 minutes or until broccoli is almost tender. Add tomato and simmer 2 minutes.

4. Spoon vegetable mixture into 1½-quart casserole; top with bread crumb mixture. Broil 1½ minutes or until crumbs are golden and cheese is melted.   *Makes 6 servings*

Broccoli Casserole with Crumb Topping

Swiss-Style Vegetables

³/4 **cup cubed unpeeled red potato**
2 **cups broccoli florets**
1 **cup cauliflower florets**
2 **teaspoons butter**
1 **cup sliced mushrooms**
1 **tablespoon all-purpose flour**
1 **cup half-and-half**
¹/2 **cup shredded Swiss cheese**
¹/4 **teaspoon salt**
¹/4 **teaspoon black pepper**
¹/4 **teaspoon hot pepper sauce (optional)**
¹/8 **teaspoon ground nutmeg**
¹/4 **cup grated Parmesan cheese**

1. *Place potato in medium saucepan; cover with cold water. Bring water to a boil. Reduce heat; cover and simmer 10 minutes. Add broccoli and cauliflower; cover and cook about 5 minutes or until all vegetables are tender. Drain; remove vegetables and set aside.*

2. *Melt butter in same saucepan over medium-low heat. Add mushrooms. Cook and stir 2 minutes. Stir in flour; cook 1 minute. Slowly stir in half-and-half; cook and stir until mixture thickens. Remove from heat. Add Swiss cheese, stirring until melted. Stir in salt, pepper, hot pepper sauce, if desired, and nutmeg.*

3. *Preheat broiler. Spray small shallow casserole with nonstick cooking spray.*

4. *Arrange vegetables in single layer in prepared casserole. Spoon sauce mixture over vegetables; sprinkle with Parmesan cheese.*

5. *Place casserole under broiler until cheese melts and browns, about 1 minute.*   *Makes 6 servings*

Swiss-Style Vegetables

Country Green Beans with Turkey-Ham

    2 teaspoons olive oil
  1/4 cup minced onion
    1 clove garlic, minced
    1 pound fresh green beans, rinsed and drained
    1 cup chopped fresh tomatoes
    6 slices (2 ounces) thinly sliced smoked
       turkey-ham
    1 tablespoon chopped fresh marjoram
    2 teaspoons chopped fresh basil
  1/8 teaspoon black pepper
  1/4 cup herbed croutons

1. Heat oil in medium saucepan over medium heat. Add onion and garlic; cook and stir about 3 minutes or until onion is tender. Reduce heat to low.

2. Add green beans, tomatoes, turkey-ham, marjoram, basil and pepper. Cook about 10 minutes, stirring occasionally, until liquid is absorbed.

3. Transfer to serving dish; top with croutons.   *Makes 4 servings*

Honeyed Beets

  1/4 cup unsweetened apple juice
    2 tablespoons cider vinegar
    1 tablespoon honey
    2 teaspoons cornstarch
    2 cans (8 ounces each) sliced beets, drained
       Salt
       Black pepper

1. Cook apple juice, vinegar, honey and cornstarch in large nonstick saucepan over medium heat until simmering.

2. Stir in beets and season to taste with salt and pepper; simmer 3 minutes.   *Makes 4 servings*

Country Green Beans with Turkey-Ham

Quick Breads

Cranberry Cheesecake Muffins

> 1 package (3 ounces) cream cheese, softened
> 4 tablespoons sugar, divided
> 1 cup milk
> 1/3 cup vegetable oil
> 1 egg
> 1 package (about 15 ounces) cranberry quick
>   bread mix

1. Preheat oven to 400°F. Grease 12 standard (2½-inch) muffin cups.

2. Beat cream cheese and 2 tablespoons sugar in small bowl until well blended; set aside.

3. Beat milk, oil and egg in large bowl until blended. Stir in quick bread mix just until dry ingredients are moistened.

4. Fill prepared muffin cups ¼ full with batter. Drop 1 teaspoon cream cheese mixture into center of each cup. Spoon remaining batter over cream cheese mixture. Sprinkle batter with remaining 2 tablespoons sugar.

5. Bake 17 to 22 minutes or until golden brown. Cool 5 minutes. Remove from muffin cups to wire rack; cool completely.

Makes 12 muffins

Prep and Bake Time: 30 minutes

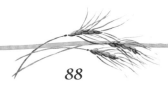

Cranberry Cheesecake Muffins

Cheddar-Apple Bread

2 cups all-purpose flour
2 teaspoons baking powder
1 teaspoon baking soda
$1/4$ teaspoon salt
1 cup packed light brown sugar
$1/2$ cup (1 stick) butter, softened
2 eggs
1 teaspoon vanilla
1 cup sour cream
$1/4$ cup milk
$1^1/2$ cups diced dried apples
1 cup (4 ounces) shredded Cheddar cheese

1. Preheat oven to 350°F. Spray 9×5-inch loaf pan with nonstick cooking spray; set aside.

2. Combine flour, baking powder, baking soda and salt in small bowl. Beat sugar and butter in large bowl with electric mixer at medium speed until light and fluffy. Beat in eggs and vanilla until blended. Add flour mixture to butter mixture alternately with sour cream and milk, beginning and ending with flour mixture. Stir in apples and cheese until blended. Spoon into prepared pan.

3. Bake 50 to 55 minutes or until toothpick inserted into center comes out clean. Cool in pan on wire rack 15 minutes. Remove from pan and cool completely on wire rack.   *Makes 12 servings*

Tip: Brown sugar can become hard during storage making it difficult to measure. To soften it, place the brown sugar in a microwavable bowl and microwave at HIGH 30 to 60 seconds or until softened.

Cheddar-Apple Bread

Calico Bell Pepper Muffins

$^1/_4$ **cup each finely chopped red, yellow and green bell pepper**
2 **tablespoons margarine**
2 **cups all-purpose flour**
4 **tablespoons sugar**
1 **tablespoon baking powder**
$^3/_4$ **teaspoon salt**
$^1/_2$ **teaspoon dried basil leaves**
1 **cup low-fat milk**
1 **whole egg**
2 **egg whites**

Preheat oven to 400°F. Paper-line 12 muffin cups or spray with cooking spray. In small skillet, cook peppers in margarine over medium-high heat until color is bright and peppers are tender-crisp, about 3 minutes. Set aside.

In large bowl, combine flour, sugar, baking powder, salt and basil. In small bowl, combine milk, whole egg and egg whites until blended. Add milk mixture and peppers with drippings to flour mixture and stir until just moistened. Spoon into prepared muffin cups. Bake 15 minutes or until golden and wooden pick inserted in centers comes out clean. Cool briefly and remove from pan.   Makes 12 muffins

Favorite recipe from **The Sugar Association, Inc.**

Calico Bell Pepper Muffins

Old-Fashioned Cake Doughnuts

3¾ cups all-purpose flour
 1 tablespoon baking powder
 1 teaspoon ground cinnamon
 ¾ teaspoon salt
 ½ teaspoon ground nutmeg
 3 eggs
 ¾ cup granulated sugar
 1 cup applesauce
 2 tablespoons butter, melted
 2 cups sifted powdered sugar
 3 tablespoons milk
 ½ teaspoon vanilla
 1 quart vegetable oil
   Colored sprinkles (optional)

1. Combine flour, baking powder, cinnamon, salt and nutmeg in medium bowl. Beat eggs in large bowl with electric mixer at high speed until frothy. Gradually beat in granulated sugar 4 minutes or until thick and lemon colored. Reduce speed to low; beat in applesauce and butter.

2. Beat in flour mixture until well blended. Divide dough in half. Pat each half into 5-inch square; wrap in plastic wrap. Refrigerate 3 hours or until well chilled.

3. To prepare glaze, stir together powdered sugar, milk and vanilla in small bowl until smooth. Cover; set aside.

4. Roll out 1 dough half to ⅜-inch thickness. Cut dough with floured 3-inch doughnut cutter; repeat with remaining dough. Reserve doughnut holes. Reroll scraps; cut dough again. Pour oil into large Dutch oven. Heat oil over medium heat until deep-fry thermometer registers 375°F. Adjust heat as necessary to maintain temperature.

5. Cook doughnuts and holes in batches 2 minutes or until golden brown, turning often. Remove with slotted spoon; drain on paper towels. Spread glaze over warm doughnuts; decorate with sprinkles, if desired.

Makes 12 doughnuts and holes

Old-Fashioned Cake Doughnuts

Country Buttermilk Biscuits

2 cups all-purpose flour
1 tablespoon baking powder
2 teaspoons sugar
1/2 teaspoon baking soda
1/2 teaspoon salt
1/3 cup shortening
2/3 cup buttermilk or sour milk*

To sour milk, place 2½ teaspoons lemon juice plus enough milk to equal ⅔ cup in 1-cup measure. Stir; let stand 5 minutes before using.

1. *Preheat oven to 450°F.*

2. *Combine flour, baking powder, sugar, baking soda and salt in medium bowl. Cut in shortening with pastry blender or two knives until mixture resembles coarse crumbs. Make well in center of dry ingredients. Add buttermilk; stir until mixture forms soft dough that clings together and forms ball.*

3. *Turn out dough onto well-floured surface. Knead dough gently 10 to 12 times. Roll or pat dough to ½-inch thickness. Cut out dough with floured 2½-inch biscuit cutter.*

4. *Place biscuits 2 inches apart on ungreased baking sheet. Bake 8 to 10 minutes or until tops and bottoms are golden brown. Serve warm.*

Makes about 9 biscuits

Drop Biscuits: *Prepare Country Buttermilk Biscuits as directed in steps 1 and 2, except increase buttermilk to 1 cup. Stir batter with wooden spoon about 15 strokes. Do not knead. Drop dough by heaping tablespoonfuls, 1 inch apart, onto greased baking sheets. Bake as directed in step 4. Makes about 18 biscuits.*

Sour Cream Dill Biscuits: *Prepare Country Buttermilk Biscuits as directed in steps 1 through 2, except omit buttermilk. Combine ½ cup sour cream, ⅓ cup milk and 1 tablespoon chopped fresh dill or 1 teaspoon dried dill weed in small bowl until well blended. Stir into dry ingredients and continue as directed in steps 3 and 4. Makes about 9 biscuits.*

continued on page 98

Country Buttermilk Biscuits

Country Buttermilk Biscuits, continued

Bacon 'n' Onion Biscuits: *Prepare Country Buttermilk Biscuits as directed in steps 1 through 2, except add 4 slices crumbled crisp-cooked bacon (about 1/3 cup) and 1/3 cup chopped green onions (about 3 onions) to flour-shortening mixture before adding buttermilk. Continue as directed in steps 3 and 4. Makes about 9 biscuits.*

Date Nut Bread

> 2 **cups all-purpose flour**
> 1/2 **cup packed light brown sugar**
> 1 **tablespoon baking powder**
> 1/2 **teaspoon salt**
> 1/4 **cup (1/2 stick) cold butter**
> 1 **cup toasted chopped walnuts**
> 1 **cup chopped dates**
> 1 1/4 **cups milk**
> 1 **egg**
> 1/2 **teaspoon grated lemon peel**

1. Preheat oven to 375°F. Spray 9×5-inch loaf pan with nonstick cooking spray; set aside.

2. Combine flour, brown sugar, baking powder and salt in large bowl. Cut in butter with pastry blender or two knives until mixture resembles fine crumbs. Add walnuts and dates; stir until coated. Beat milk, egg and lemon peel in small bowl with fork. Add to flour mixture; stir just until moistened. Pour into prepared pan.

3. Bake 45 to 50 minutes or until toothpick inserted into center comes out clean. Cool in pan on wire rack 10 minutes. Remove from pan and cool completely on wire rack.   *Makes 12 servings*

Tip: *Dates can be chopped with a chef's knife or cut into small pieces using kitchen shears. Lightly spray the knife or shears with nonstick cooking spray to prevent the dates from sticking.*

Honey Soda Bread

2 cups all-purpose flour
1 cup whole wheat flour
2 teaspoons baking soda
$^1/_2$ teaspoon salt
$^1/_4$ cup butter or margarine, cut up
1 cup golden raisins
2 teaspoons caraway seeds
1 cup plain low-fat yogurt
$^1/_3$ cup honey
2 tablespoons milk

In large bowl, combine flours, baking soda and salt; mix well. Cut in butter until mixture resembles coarse crumbs; mix in raisins and caraway seeds.

In small bowl, whisk together yogurt and honey. Add to flour mixture; stir until just combined. Turn dough onto lightly floured surface; knead 10 times or until dough is smooth. Form dough into ball; place on lightly greased baking sheet. With sharp knife, cut an "X" $^1/_4$ inch deep into top of loaf; brush with milk. Bake at 325°F for 45 to 50 minutes, or until golden. Cool on wire rack.   Makes 1 loaf

Favorite recipe from **National Honey Board**

Note: Whole wheat flour is more perishable than other types of flour, so purchase it in small amounts and store it in the refrigerator for no more than 3 months. Allow chilled flour to return to room temperature before using it.

Ham and Cheese Corn Muffins

1 package (about 8 ounces) corn muffin mix
$^1/_2$ cup chopped deli ham
$^1/_2$ cup (2 ounces) shredded Swiss cheese
$^1/_3$ cup milk
1 egg
1 tablespoon Dijon mustard

1. *Preheat oven to 400°F. Line 9 standard (2½-inch) muffin cups with paper baking cups.*

2. *Combine muffin mix, ham and cheese in medium bowl. Beat milk, egg and mustard in 1-cup glass measure. Stir milk mixture into dry ingredients just until moistened.*

3. *Fill muffin cups two-thirds full. Bake 18 to 20 minutes or until light golden brown. Remove muffin pan to cooling rack. Let stand 5 minutes. Serve muffins warm.*   *Makes 9 muffins*

Prep and Cook Time: *30 minutes*

Serving Suggestion: *For added flavor, serve Ham and Cheese Corn Muffins with honey-flavored butter. To prepare, stir together equal amounts of honey and softened butter.*

Tip: *When making muffin batter, stir just until the dry ingredients are moistened. The batter will be lumpy, but the lumps will disappear during baking. Overmixing will result in muffins with a tough texture.*

Ham and Cheese Corn Muffins

Cherry Zucchini Bread

2 eggs
3/4 cup sugar
1/3 cup vegetable oil
1/3 cup lemon juice
1/4 cup water
2 cups all-purpose flour
2 teaspoons baking powder
1 teaspoon ground cinnamon
1/2 teaspoon baking soda
1/4 teaspoon salt
2/3 cup shredded unpeeled zucchini
2/3 cup dried tart cherries
1 tablespoon grated lemon peel

Put eggs in large mixing bowl. Beat with an electric mixer on medium speed 3 to 4 minutes or until eggs are thick and lemon colored. Add sugar, oil, lemon juice and water; mix well. Combine flour, baking powder, cinnamon, baking soda and salt. Add flour mixture to egg mixture; mix well. Stir in zucchini, cherries and lemon peel.

Grease and flour bottom of 8½×4½-inch loaf pan. Pour batter into prepared pan. Bake in preheated 350°F oven 55 to 65 minutes or until wooden toothpick inserted in center comes out clean. Let cool in pan on wire rack 10 minutes. Loosen edges with a metal spatula. Remove from pan. Let cool completely. Wrap tightly in plastic wrap and store in refrigerator.   *Makes 1 loaf, about 16 servings*

Favorite recipe from **Cherry Marketing Institute**

Cherry Zucchini Bread

Grandma's® Bran Muffins

2½ cups bran flakes, divided
1 cup raisins
1 cup boiling water
2 cups buttermilk
1 cup GRANDMA'S® Molasses
½ cup canola oil
2 eggs, beaten
2¾ cups all-purpose flour
2½ teaspoons baking soda
½ teaspoon salt

Heat oven to 400°F. In medium bowl, mix 1 cup bran flakes, raisins and water. Set aside. In large bowl, combine remaining ingredients. Stir in bran-raisin mixture. Pour into greased muffin pan cups. Fill ⅔ full and bake for 20 minutes. Remove muffins and place on rack to cool. *Makes 48 muffins*

Peach and Sausage Waffles

½ pound BOB EVANS® Original Recipe Roll Sausage
1 cup all-purpose flour
3 tablespoons sugar
2 teaspoons baking powder
2 eggs
2 cups milk
4 tablespoons melted butter
1 cup chopped, drained canned peaches

Preheat waffle iron. If preparing waffles in advance, preheat oven to 200°F. Crumble and cook sausage in medium skillet until browned; drain on paper towels. Whisk flour, sugar and baking powder in large bowl. Whisk eggs and milk in medium bowl until well blended. Pour liquid ingredients over dry ingredients; whisk until just combined. Stir in butter until blended. Stir in peaches and sausage. Lightly butter grids of waffle iron; add ½ cup batter to hot iron. Cook waffles according to manufacturer's instructions. Serve immediately or hold in oven until ready to serve. *Makes 6 servings*

Grandma's® Bran Muffins

Buttermilk Cornbread Loaf

1½ cups all-purpose flour
1 cup yellow cornmeal
⅓ cup sugar
2 teaspoons baking powder
1 teaspoon salt
½ teaspoon baking soda
½ cup shortening
1⅓ cups buttermilk*
2 eggs

*To sour milk, place 4 teaspoons lemon juice plus enough milk to equal 1⅓ cups in 2-cup measure. Stir; let stand 5 minutes before using.

1. Preheat oven to 375°F. Grease 8×4-inch loaf pan; set aside.

2. Combine flour, cornmeal, sugar, baking powder, salt and baking soda in medium bowl. Cut in shortening with pastry blender or two knives until mixture resembles coarse crumbs.

3. Whisk buttermilk and eggs in small bowl. Make well in center of dry ingredients. Add buttermilk mixture; stir until mixture forms stiff batter. (Batter will be lumpy.) Turn into prepared pan; spread mixture evenly, removing any air bubbles.

4. Bake 50 to 55 minutes or until toothpick inserted in center comes out clean. Cool in pan on wire rack 10 minutes. Remove from pan; cool on rack 10 minutes more. Serve warm. *Makes 1 loaf*

Buttermilk Cornbread Loaf

Cakes and Pies

Hershey's Red Velvet Cake

$^{1}/_{2}$ cup (1 stick) butter or margarine, softened
1$^{1}/_{2}$ cups sugar
  2 eggs
  1 teaspoon vanilla extract
  1 cup buttermilk
  2 tablespoons (1-ounce bottle) red food color
  2 cups all-purpose flour
$^{1}/_{3}$ cup HERSHEY'S Cocoa
  1 teaspoon salt
1$^{1}/_{2}$ teaspoons baking soda
  1 tablespoon white vinegar
  1 can (16 ounces) ready-to-spread vanilla frosting
    HERSHEY'S MINI CHIPS™ Semi-Sweet Chocolate
    Chips or HERSHEY'S Milk Chocolate Chips
    (optional)

1. Heat oven to 350°F. Grease and flour 13×9×2-inch baking pan.

2. Beat butter and sugar in large bowl; add eggs and vanilla, beating well. Stir together buttermilk and food color. Stir together flour, cocoa and salt; add alternately to butter mixture with buttermilk mixture, mixing well. Stir in baking soda and vinegar. Pour into prepared pan.

3. Bake 30 to 35 minutes or until wooden pick inserted in center comes out clean. Cool completely in pan on wire rack. Frost; garnish with chocolate chips, if desired.   *Makes about 15 servings*

Hershey's Red Velvet Cake

Deep-Dish Peach Custard Pie

3¹/₂ cups (about 7 medium) peeled, pitted and sliced
    peaches
  1 unbaked 9-inch (4-cup volume) deep-dish pie
    shell
  1 can (14 ounces) NESTLÉ® CARNATION®
    Sweetened Condensed Milk
  2 large eggs
¹/₄ cup butter or margarine, melted
  1 to 3 teaspoons lemon juice
¹/₂ teaspoon ground cinnamon
    Dash ground nutmeg
    Streusel Topping (recipe follows)

PREHEAT oven to 425°F.

ARRANGE peaches in pie shell. Combine sweetened condensed milk, eggs, butter, lemon juice, cinnamon and nutmeg in large mixer bowl; beat until smooth. Pour over peaches.

BAKE for 10 minutes. Sprinkle with Streusel Topping. Reduce oven temperature to 350°F; bake for additional 55 to 60 minutes or until knife inserted near center comes out clean. Cool on wire rack.

Makes 8 servings

Streusel Topping: **COMBINE** ¹/₃ cup packed brown sugar, ¹/₃ cup all-purpose flour and ¹/₃ cup chopped walnuts in medium bowl. Cut in 2 tablespoons butter or margarine with pastry blender or two knives until mixture resembles coarse crumbs.

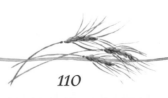

Deep-Dish Peach Custard Pie

Toffee-Topped Pineapple Upside-Down Cakes

¼ **cup light corn syrup**
¼ **cup (½ stick) butter or margarine, melted**
1 **cup HEATH® BITS 'O BRICKLE® or SKOR® English Toffee Bits**
4 **pineapple rings**
4 **maraschino cherries**
¼ **cup (½ stick) butter or margarine, softened**
⅔ **cup sugar**
1 **egg**
1 **tablespoon rum or 1 teaspoon rum extract**
1⅓ **cups all-purpose flour**
2 **teaspoons baking powder**
⅔ **cup milk**

1. Heat oven to 350°F. Lightly coat inside of 4 individual 2-cup baking dishes with vegetable oil spray.

2. Stir together 1 tablespoon corn syrup and 1 tablespoon melted butter in each of 4 baking dishes. Sprinkle each with ¼ cup toffee. Center pineapple rings on toffee and place cherries in centers.

3. Beat softened butter and sugar in small bowl until blended. Add egg and rum, beating well. Stir together flour and baking powder; add alternately with milk to butter-sugar mixture, beating until smooth. Spoon about ¾ cup batter into each prepared dish.

4. Bake 25 to 30 minutes or until wooden pick inserted in centers comes out clean. Immediately invert onto serving dish. Refrigerate leftovers. *Makes 4 (4-inch) cakes*

Toffee-Topped Pineapple Upside-Down Cakes

Pumpkin Carrot Cake

2 cups all-purpose flour
2 teaspoons baking soda
2 teaspoons ground cinnamon
$^1\!/_2$ teaspoon salt
$^3\!/_4$ cup milk
$1^1\!/_2$ teaspoons lemon juice
3 eggs
$1^1\!/_4$ cups LIBBY'S® 100% Pure Pumpkin
$1^1\!/_2$ cups granulated sugar
$^1\!/_2$ cup packed brown sugar
$^1\!/_2$ cup vegetable oil
1 can (8 ounces) crushed pineapple, drained
1 cup (about 3 medium) grated carrots
1 cup flaked coconut
$1^1\!/_4$ cups chopped nuts, divided
Cream Cheese Frosting (recipe follows)

PREHEAT oven to 350°F. Grease two 9-inch round baking pans.

COMBINE flour, baking soda, cinnamon and salt in small bowl. Combine milk and lemon juice in liquid measuring cup (mixture will appear curdled).

BEAT eggs, pumpkin, granulated sugar, brown sugar, oil, pineapple, carrots and milk mixture in large mixer bowl; mix well. Gradually add flour mixture; beat until combined. Stir in coconut and 1 cup nuts. Pour into prepared baking pans.

BAKE for 30 to 35 minutes or until wooden pick inserted in center comes out clean. Cool in pans for 15 minutes. Remove to wire racks to cool completely.

FROST between layers, on side and top of cake with Cream Cheese Frosting. Garnish with remaining nuts. Store in refrigerator.

Makes 12 servings

Cream Cheese Frosting: **COMBINE** 11 ounces softened cream cheese, $^1\!/_3$ cup softened butter and $3^1\!/_2$ cups sifted powdered sugar in large mixer bowl until fluffy. Add 1 teaspoon vanilla extract, 2 teaspoons orange juice and 1 teaspoon grated orange peel; beat until combined.

Pumpkin Carrot Cake

Zesty Lemon Pound Cake

1 cup (6 ounces) NESTLÉ® TOLL HOUSE® Premier
    White Morsels or 3 bars (6-ounce box)
    NESTLÉ® TOLL HOUSE® Premier White Baking
    Bars, broken into pieces
2¹/₂ cups all-purpose flour
1 teaspoon baking powder
¹/₂ teaspoon salt
1 cup (2 sticks) butter, softened
1¹/₂ cups granulated sugar
2 teaspoons vanilla extract
3 eggs
3 to 4 tablespoons grated lemon peel
    (about 3 medium lemons)
1¹/₃ cups buttermilk
1 cup powdered sugar
3 tablespoons fresh lemon juice

PREHEAT *oven to 350°F. Grease and flour 12-cup bundt pan.*

MELT *morsels in medium, uncovered, microwave-safe bowl on MEDIUM-HIGH (70%) power for 1 minute. STIR. Morsels may retain some of their original shape. If necessary, microwave at additional 10- to 15-second intervals, stirring just until morsels are melted. Cool slightly.*

COMBINE *flour, baking powder and salt in small bowl. Beat butter, granulated sugar and vanilla extract in large mixer bowl until creamy. Beat in eggs, one at a time, beating well after each addition. Beat in lemon peel and melted morsels. Gradually beat in flour mixture alternately with buttermilk. Pour into prepared bundt pan.*

BAKE *for 50 to 55 minutes or until wooden pick inserted in cake comes out clean. Cool in pan on wire rack for 10 minutes. Combine powdered sugar and lemon juice in small bowl. Make holes in cake with wooden pick; pour half of lemon glaze over cake. Let stand for 5 minutes. Invert onto plate. Make holes in top of cake; pour remaining glaze over cake. Cool completely before serving.*

Makes 16 servings

Zesty Lemon Pound Cake

Apple-Scotch Snack Cake

Topping
    $^2/_3$ cup quick or old fashioned oats
    6 tablespoons all-purpose flour
    4 tablespoons butter, softened
    3 tablespoons firmly packed brown sugar

Cake
    $2^1/_4$ cups all-purpose flour
    1 cup quick or old fashioned oats
    1 tablespoon baking powder
    $^1/_2$ teaspoon salt
    1 cup firmly packed brown sugar
    2 eggs
    $1^1/_4$ cups milk
    6 tablespoons butter, melted and cooled
    1 teaspoon vanilla extract
    $1^1/_3$ cups peeled and finely chopped apples
        (about 2 small tart apples)
    $1^1/_3$ cups NESTLÉ® TOLL HOUSE® Butterscotch
        Flavored Morsels, divided
    $1^1/_2$ teaspoons milk
    Vanilla ice cream (optional)

PREHEAT oven to 350°F. Grease bottom of 13×9-inch baking pan.

For Topping
COMBINE oats, flour, butter and brown sugar in small bowl. With clean fingers, mix until crumbly; set aside.

For Cake
COMBINE flour, oats, baking powder and salt in large bowl. Combine brown sugar and eggs with wire whisk. Whisk in $1^1/_4$ cups milk, melted butter and vanilla extract. Add to flour mixture all at once; add apples. Stir gently until just combined. Pour into pan. Sprinkle with 1 cup morsels; crumble topping evenly over morsels.

BAKE for 40 minutes or until golden brown and wooden pick inserted in center comes out with a few moist crumbs clinging to it. Remove from oven to wire rack. Microwave remaining $^1/_3$ cup morsels and $1^1/_2$ teaspoons milk in small microwave-safe bowl. Microwave on

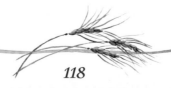

HIGH (100%) power for 20 seconds; stir until smooth. Carefully drizzle over hot cake in pan. Cool in pan at least 30 minutes. Cut into squares; serve warm or at room temperature with ice cream. Store tightly covered at room temperature.   *Makes 16 servings*

Sour Cream Cherry Cake

   1 **(9-ounce) package yellow cake mix**
   1 **egg**
1¹/₂ **cups reduced-fat (2%) milk, divided**
   1 **(3¹/₂-ounce) package vanilla pudding mix**
  ¹/₂ **cup dairy sour cream**
  ¹/₂ **teaspoon grated lemon peel**
   2 **cups pitted Northwest fresh sweet cherries**
   2 **tablespoons currant jelly, melted**
     Mint sprigs
   1 **cup sweetened whipped cream (optional)**

Prepare yellow cake according to package directions using egg and ¹/₂ cup milk. Pour batter into flan pan and bake according to package directions. Prepare vanilla pudding according to package directions using 1 cup milk; remove from heat and stir in sour cream and lemon peel. When cake is cool, fill with vanilla pudding. Top with cherries; brush with melted jelly. Garnish with mint. Serve with whipped cream, if desired.   *Makes 8 servings*

Favorite recipe from **Northwest Cherry Growers**

Desserts

Chilled Cherry Cheesecake

4 chocolate graham crackers, crushed
  (1 cup crumbs)
12 ounces cream cheese
8 ounces vanilla yogurt
1/4 cup sugar
1 teaspoon vanilla
1 envelope unflavored gelatin
1/4 cup cold water
1 can (20 ounces) cherry pie filling

1. Sprinkle cracker crumbs on bottom of 8-inch square baking pan. Beat cream cheese, yogurt, sugar and vanilla in medium bowl with electric mixer at medium speed until smooth and creamy.

2. Sprinkle gelatin into water in small cup; let stand 2 minutes. Microwave at HIGH 40 seconds, stir and let stand 2 minutes or until gelatin is completely dissolved.

3. Gradually beat gelatin mixture into cheese mixture with electric mixer until well blended. Pour into prepared pan; refrigerate until firm. Spoon cherry topping onto cheesecake. Refrigerate until ready to serve. *Makes 9 servings*

Chilled Cherry Cheesecake

Lemon Cake-Top Pudding

1/4 **cup sliced natural almonds**
4 **eggs, separated**
1 **cup sugar**
3 **tablespoons margarine, softened**
3 **tablespoons all-purpose flour**
1/8 **teaspoon salt**
1/3 **cup freshly squeezed SUNKIST® lemon juice**
1 **cup reduced-fat or lowfat milk**
   Grated peel of 1/2 SUNKIST® lemon

Preheat oven to 325°F. Spray the inside of 1½-quart glass casserole with butter-flavored nonstick cooking spray. Sprinkle almonds over bottom of casserole. In medium bowl, with electric mixer, beat egg whites at high speed until soft peaks form. Gradually add 1/4 cup sugar, beating until medium-stiff peaks form; set aside. With same beaters, in large bowl, beat together margarine and remaining 3/4 cup sugar. With same beaters, in small bowl, beat egg yolks well; add to margarine-sugar mixture, beating thoroughly. Add flour, salt and lemon juice; beat well. Stir in milk and lemon peel until blended. Stir in 1/3 of the egg white mixture, then gently fold in remaining egg whites. Pour batter into prepared casserole over almonds. Place casserole in shallow baking pan filled with 1 inch hot water. Bake, uncovered, for 50 to 55 minutes, or until golden brown and top springs back when lightly touched with finger. Carefully remove from water and let set for 20 to 30 minutes. Serve warm or chilled. Garnish each serving with lemon half-cartwheel slices and fresh mint leaves, if desired. *Makes 6 to 8 servings*

Lemon Cake-Top Pudding

Toffee Bread Pudding with Cinnamon Toffee Sauce

   3 **cups milk**
   4 **eggs**
   ³/₄ **cup sugar**
   ³/₄ **teaspoon ground cinnamon**
   ³/₄ **teaspoon vanilla extract**
   ¹/₂ **teaspoon salt**
   6 **to 6¹/₂ cups ¹/₂-inch cubes French, Italian or
        sourdough bread**
   1 **cup SKOR® English Toffee Bits or HEATH®
        BITS 'O BRICKLE® Almond Toffee Bits, divided
        Cinnamon Toffee Sauce (recipe follows)
        Sweetened whipped cream or ice cream
        (optional)**

1. *Heat oven to 350°F. Butter 13×9×2-inch baking pan.*

2. *Mix together milk, eggs, sugar, cinnamon, vanilla and salt in large bowl with wire whisk. Stir in bread cubes, coating completely. Allow to stand 10 minutes. Stir in ¹/₂ cup toffee bits. Pour into prepared pan. Sprinkle remaining ¹/₂ cup toffee bits over surface.*

3. *Bake 40 to 45 minutes or until surface is set. Cool 30 minutes.*

4. *Meanwhile, prepare Cinnamon Toffee Sauce. Cut pudding into squares; top with sauce and sweetened whipped cream or ice cream, if desired.* Makes 12 servings

Cinnamon Toffee Sauce: *Combine ³/₄ cup SKOR® English Toffee Bits or HEATH® BITS 'O BRICKLE® Almond Toffee Bits, ¹/₃ cup whipping cream and ¹/₈ teaspoon ground cinnamon in medium saucepan. Cook over low heat, stirring constantly, until toffee melts and mixture is well blended. (As toffee melts, small bits of almond will remain.) Makes about ²/₃ cup sauce.*

Note: *This dessert is best eaten the same day it is prepared.*

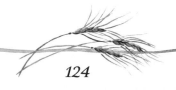

Toffee Bread Pudding with Cinnamon Toffee Sauce

Banana Pudding

60 to 70 vanilla wafers*
 1 cup granulated sugar
 3 tablespoons cornstarch
 ¼ teaspoon salt
 2 cans (12 fluid ounces each) NESTLÉ®
   CARNATION® Evaporated Milk
 2 eggs, lightly beaten
 3 tablespoons butter, cut into pieces
1½ teaspoons vanilla extract
 5 ripe but firm large bananas, cut into ¼-inch
   slices
 1 container (8 ounces) frozen whipped topping,
   thawed

*A 12-ounce box of vanilla wafers contains about 88 wafers.

LINE bottom and side of 2½-quart glass bowl with about 40 wafers.

COMBINE sugar, cornstarch and salt in medium saucepan. Gradually stir in evaporated milk to dissolve cornstarch. Whisk in eggs. Add butter. Cook over medium heat, stirring constantly, until the mixture begins to thicken. Reduce heat to low; bring to a simmer and cook for 1 minute, stirring constantly. Remove from heat. Stir in vanilla extract. Let cool slightly.

POUR half of pudding over wafers. Top with half of bananas. Layer remaining vanilla wafers over bananas. Combine remaining pudding and bananas; spoon over wafers. Refrigerate for at least 4 hours. Top with whipped topping.   Makes 8 servings

Baked Apples

2 tablespoons sugar
2 tablespoons raisins, chopped
2 tablespoons chopped walnuts
2 tablespoons GRANDMA'S® Molasses
6 apples, cored

Heat oven to 350°F. In medium bowl, combine sugar, raisins, walnuts and molasses. Fill apple cavities with molasses mixture. Place in 13×9-inch baking dish. Pour ½ cup hot water over apples and bake 25 minutes or until soft. *Makes 6 servings*

Strawberry Dessert

2 cups graham cracker crumbs
⅓ cup butter, melted
¼ cup sugar
2 packages (8 ounces each) cream cheese, softened
1 cup powdered sugar
2 containers (6 ounces each) lemon yogurt
3 pints strawberries, sliced
1 container (12 ounces) frozen whipped topping, thawed

1. Combine cracker crumbs, butter and sugar in medium bowl; mix well. Press onto bottom of 13×9-inch baking dish.

2. Beat cream cheese and powdered sugar 1 minute in medium bowl with electric mixer at medium speed. Beat in yogurt until blended. Pour mixture over crust. Arrange strawberries on cream cheese mixture. Spread whipped topping over strawberries. Chill at least 4 hours or overnight before serving. *Makes 9 to 12 servings*

Triple Chip Cheesecake

Crust
  1³/₄ **cups chocolate graham cracker crumbs**
  ¹/₃ **cup butter or margarine, melted**

Filling
  3 **packages (8 ounces each) cream cheese, softened**
  ³/₄ **cup granulated sugar**
  ¹/₂ **cup sour cream**
  3 **tablespoons all-purpose flour**
  1¹/₂ **teaspoons vanilla extract**
  3 **eggs**
  1 **cup (6 ounces) NESTLÉ® TOLL HOUSE®**
   Butterscotch Flavored Morsels
  1 **cup (6 ounces) NESTLÉ® TOLL HOUSE®**
   Semi-Sweet Chocolate Morsels
  1 **cup (6 ounces) NESTLÉ® TOLL HOUSE®**
   Premier White Morsels

Topping
  1 **tablespoon each NESTLÉ® TOLL HOUSE®**
   Butterscotch Flavored Morsels, Semi-Sweet
   Chocolate Morsels and Premier White Morsels

PREHEAT oven to 300°F. Grease 9-inch springform pan.

For Crust
COMBINE crumbs and butter in small bowl. Press onto bottom and 1 inch up side of prepared pan.

For Filling
BEAT cream cheese and granulated sugar in large mixer bowl until smooth. Add sour cream, flour and vanilla extract; mix well. Add eggs; beat on low speed until combined. Melt butterscotch morsels according to package directions. Stir until smooth. Add 1¹/₂ cups batter to melted morsels. Pour into crust. Repeat procedure with semi-sweet morsels. Carefully spoon over butterscotch layer. Melt Premier White morsels according to package directions and blend into remaining batter in mixer bowl. Carefully pour over semi-sweet layer.

continued on page 130

Triple Chip Cheesecake

Triple Chip Cheesecake, continued

BAKE *for 1 hour and 10 to 15 minutes or until center is almost set. Cool in pan on wire rack for 10 minutes. Run knife around edge of cheesecake. Let stand for 1 hour.*

For Topping
PLACE *each flavor of morsels separately into three small, heavy-duty resealable plastic food storage bags. Microwave on HIGH (100%) power for 20 seconds; knead bags to mix. Microwave at additional 10-second intervals, kneading until smooth. Cut small hole in corner of each bag; squeeze to drizzle over cheesecake. Refrigerate for at least 3 hours or overnight. Remove side of pan.*

Makes 12 to 16 servings

Winter Fruit Compote

  **1 can (16 ounces) pitted dark sweet cherries
      in syrup, undrained
  1 teaspoon cornstarch
1¹⁄₂ tablespoons honey
  1 tablespoon almond-flavored liqueur or
     ¹⁄₂ teaspoon almond extract
  2 ripe Bartlett or Comice pears, peeled, cored
     and cut into 1-inch cubes
  1 teaspoon chopped fresh mint
    Mint sprigs (optional)**

1. *Drain cherries reserving ¹⁄₄ cup liquid. Combine reserved liquid and cornstarch in small bowl; mix until smooth. Add mixture to saucepan and bring to a boil over medium-high heat; stirring frequently. Reduce heat to simmer; as mixture begins to thicken, stir in honey and liqueur.*

2. *Stir in pears and drained cherries. Cook 2 minutes or until fruit is warm, stirring occasionally. Spoon into dessert dishes; sprinkle with mint and garnish with mint sprigs. Serve warm or at room temperature.*

Makes 4 servings

Cookies and Cream Layered Dessert

1 cup cold milk
1 package (4-serving size) white chocolate instant
    pudding mix
1 package chocolate creme-filled sandwich cookies
¹/₄ (¹/₂ stick) cup butter, melted
2 packages (8 ounces each) cream cheese, softened
2 cups powdered sugar
1 container (8 ounces) frozen whipped topping,
    thawed
1 teaspoon vanilla
2 cups whipping cream

1. Whisk milk and pudding mix in medium bowl until thick. Set aside.

2. Finely crush cookies in large resealable food storage bag with rolling pin. Combine 2 cups crushed cookies and butter in small bowl. Press on bottom of 2-quart trifle dish. Reserve remaining crushed cookies.

3. Beat cream cheese and powdered sugar 2 minutes in large bowl with electric mixer at medium speed until blended. Fold in pudding mixture, whipped topping and vanilla.

4. Beat whipping cream in small deep bowl with electric mixer until soft peaks form. Fold into cream cheese mixture.

5. Spoon one third cream cheese mixture over crushed cookies. Sprinkle one third remaining cookie crumbs over cream cheese layer. Repeat layers twice. Refrigerate until ready to serve.

Makes 12 servings

Lemon Cheesecake

Crust
- 35 vanilla wafers
- ³/₄ cup slivered almonds, toasted
- ¹/₃ cup sugar
- ¹/₄ (¹/₂ stick) cup butter, melted

Filling
- 3 packages (8 ounces each) cream cheese, softened
- ³/₄ cup sugar
- 4 eggs
- ¹/₃ cup whipping cream
- 1 tablespoon grated lemon peel
- ¹/₄ cup lemon juice
- 1 teaspoon vanilla

Topping
- 1 pint strawberries
- 2 tablespoons sugar

1. Preheat oven to 375°F. For crust, combine wafers, almonds and ¹/₃ cup sugar in food processor or blender; process until fine crumbs are formed. Combine crumb mixture with melted butter in medium bowl. Press mixture evenly on bottom and 1 inch up side of 9-inch springform pan. Set aside.

2. For filling, beat cream cheese and ³/₄ cup sugar in large bowl with electric mixer at high speed 2 to 3 minutes or until fluffy. Add eggs one at a time, beating after each addition. Add whipping cream, lemon peel, lemon juice and vanilla; beat just until blended. Pour into prepared crust. Place springform pan on baking sheet. Bake 45 to 55 minutes or until set. Cool completely on wire rack. Cover and refrigerate at least 10 hours or overnight.

3. For topping, hull and slice strawberries. Combine with 2 tablespoons sugar in medium bowl. Let stand 15 minutes. Serve over cheesecake.

Makes 16 servings

Prep Time: *20 minutes*
Chill Time: *10 to 12 hours, 15 minutes*

Lemon Cheesecake

Rocky Road Brownies

1 cup miniature marshmallows
1¼ cups HERSHEY'S Semi-Sweet Chocolate Chips
½ cup chopped nuts
½ cup (1 stick) butter or margarine
1 cup sugar
2 eggs
1 teaspoon vanilla extract
½ cup all-purpose flour
⅓ cup HERSHEY'S Cocoa
½ teaspoon baking powder
½ teaspoon salt

1. Heat oven to 350°F. Grease 9-inch square baking pan.

2. Stir together marshmallows, chocolate chips and nuts; set aside. Place butter in large microwave-safe bowl. Microwave at HIGH (100% power) 1 to 1½ minutes or until melted. Add sugar, eggs and vanilla, beating with spoon until well blended. Add flour, cocoa, baking powder and salt; blend well. Spread batter in prepared pan.

3. Bake 22 minutes. Sprinkle chocolate chip mixture over top. Continue baking 5 minutes or until marshmallows have softened and puffed slightly. Cool completely. With wet knife, cut into squares.

Makes about 20 brownies

Rocky Road Brownies

Baked Apple Slices with Peanut Butter Crumble

4 cups peeled and thinly sliced apples
1 cup sugar, divided
1 cup all-purpose flour, divided
3 tablespoons butter or margarine, divided
1 cup quick-cooking or old-fashioned rolled oats
$^1/_2$ teaspoon ground cinnamon
1 cup REESE'S® Creamy or Crunchy Peanut Butter
Sweetened whipped cream or ice cream
(optional)

1. Heat oven to 350°F. Grease 9-inch square baking pan.

2. Stir together apples, $^3/_4$ cup sugar and $^1/_4$ cup flour in large bowl. Spread in prepared pan; dot with 2 tablespoons butter. Combine oats, remaining $^3/_4$ cup flour, remaining $^1/_4$ cup sugar and cinnamon in medium bowl; set aside.

3. Place remaining 1 tablespoon butter and peanut butter in small microwave-safe bowl. Microwave at HIGH (100%) 30 seconds or until butter is melted; stir until smooth. Add to oat mixture; blend until crumbs are formed. Sprinkle crumb mixture over apples.

4. Bake 40 to 45 minutes or until apples are tender and edges are bubbly. Cool slightly. Serve warm or cool with whipped cream or ice cream, if desired.　　　　　　　　　　　　Makes 6 to 8 servings

Baked Apple Slices with Peanut Butter Crumble

Berry Cobbler

2½ cups fresh raspberries*
2½ cups fresh blueberries or strawberries,* sliced
2 tablespoons cornstarch
½ to ¾ cup sugar
1 cup all-purpose flour
1½ teaspoons baking powder
¼ teaspoon salt
⅓ cup milk
⅓ cup butter or margarine, melted
2 tablespoons thawed frozen apple juice
    concentrate
¼ teaspoon ground nutmeg

One (16-ounce) bag frozen raspberries and one (16-ounce) bag frozen blueberries or strawberries can be substituted for fresh berries. Thaw berries, reserving juices. Increase cornstarch to 3 tablespoons.

1. Preheat oven to 375°F.

2. Combine berries and cornstarch in medium bowl; toss lightly to coat. Add sugar to taste; mix well. Spoon into 1½-quart or 8-inch square baking dish. Combine flour, baking powder and salt in medium bowl. Add milk, butter and juice concentrate; mix just until dry ingredients are moistened. Drop 6 heaping tablespoonfuls batter evenly over berries; sprinkle with nutmeg.

3. Bake 25 minutes or until topping is golden brown and fruit is bubbly. Cool on wire rack. Serve warm or at room temperature.

Makes 6 servings

Prep Time: *5 minutes*
Bake Time: *25 minutes*

Tip: *Cobblers are best served warm or at room temperature on the day they are made. Leftovers should be kept covered and refrigerated for up to two days. Reheat them, covered, in a 350°F oven until warm.*

Berry Cobbler

Ambrosia

1 can (20 ounces) DOLE® Pineapple Chunks,
    drained
1 can (11 or 15 ounces) DOLE® Mandarin Oranges,
    drained
1 DOLE® Banana, sliced
1¹/₂ cups seedless grapes
¹/₂ cup miniature marshmallows
1 cup vanilla lowfat yogurt
¹/₄ cup flaked coconut, toasted

• Combine pineapple chunks, mandarin oranges, banana, grapes and marshmallows in medium bowl.

• Stir yogurt into fruit mixture. Sprinkle with coconut.

Makes 4 to 6 servings

Prep Time: *15 minutes*

Tip: To toast the coconut for the Ambrosia, spread it evenly on an ungreased cookie sheet. Bake in a preheated 375°F oven 5 to 7 minutes, stirring occasionally, until light golden brown.

Ambrosia

Cookies and Bars

Layered Cookie Bars

³/₄ cup (1¹/₂ sticks) butter or margarine
1³/₄ cups vanilla wafer crumbs
6 tablespoons HERSHEY'S Cocoa
¹/₄ cup sugar
1 can (14 ounces) sweetened condensed milk
1 cup HERSHEY'S Semi-Sweet Chocolate Chips
³/₄ cup SKOR® English Toffee Bits
1 cup chopped walnuts

1. Heat oven to 350°F. Melt butter in 13×9×2-inch baking pan in oven. Combine crumbs, cocoa and sugar; sprinkle over butter.

2. Pour sweetened condensed milk evenly on top of crumbs. Top with chocolate chips and toffee bits, then nuts; press down firmly.

3. Bake 25 to 30 minutes or until lightly browned. Cool completely in pan on wire rack. Chill, if desired. Cut into bars. Store covered at room temperature.

Makes about 36 bars

Layered Cookie Bars

Pumpkin Spiced and Iced Cookies

2¼ cups all-purpose flour
1½ teaspoons pumpkin pie spice
1 teaspoon baking powder
½ teaspoon baking soda
½ teaspoon salt
1 cup (2 sticks) butter or margarine, softened
1 cup granulated sugar
1 can (15 ounces) LIBBY'S® 100% Pure Pumpkin
2 eggs
1 teaspoon vanilla extract
2 cups (12-ounce package) NESTLÉ® TOLL HOUSE®
   Semi-Sweet Chocolate Morsels
1 cup chopped walnuts (optional)
   Vanilla Glaze (recipe follows)

PREHEAT oven to 375°F. Grease baking sheets.

COMBINE flour, pumpkin pie spice, baking powder, baking soda and salt in medium bowl. Beat butter and granulated sugar in large mixer bowl until creamy. Beat in pumpkin, eggs and vanilla extract. Gradually beat in flour mixture. Stir in morsels and nuts. Drop by rounded tablespoon onto prepared baking sheets.

BAKE for 15 to 20 minutes or until edges are lightly browned. Cool on baking sheets for 2 minutes; remove to wire rack to cool completely. Spread or drizzle with Vanilla Glaze.

Makes about 5½ dozen cookies

Vanilla Glaze: **COMBINE** 1 cup powdered sugar, 1 to 1½ tablespoons milk and ½ teaspoon vanilla extract in small bowl; mix well.

Pumpkin Spiced and Iced Cookies

Dad's Ginger Molasses Cookies

1 cup sugar
1 cup shortening
1 tablespoon baking soda
2 teaspoons ground ginger
2 teaspoons ground cinnamon
1 teaspoon ground cloves
$^1/_2$ teaspoon salt
1 cup molasses
$^2/_3$ cup double-strength instant coffee*
1 egg
$4^3/_4$ cups all-purpose flour

*To prepare double-strength coffee, follow instructions for instant coffee but use twice the recommended amount of instant coffee granules.

1. Preheat oven to 350°F. Lightly grease cookie sheets.

2. Beat sugar and shortening with electric mixer at medium speed until creamy. Beat in baking soda, ginger, cinnamon, cloves and salt until well blended. Beat molasses, coffee and egg. Gradually add flour, beating on low speed just until blended.

3. Drop dough by rounded tablespoonfuls 2 inches apart on prepared cookie sheets. Bake 12 to 15 minutes or until cookies are set but not browned. Cool on cookie sheets 1 minute. Remove to wire racks; cool completely.   *Makes about 6 dozen cookies*

Dad's Ginger Molasses Cookies

Pfeffernüesse

3½ cups all-purpose flour
2 teaspoons baking powder
1½ teaspoons ground cinnamon
1 teaspoon ground ginger
½ teaspoon baking soda
½ teaspoon salt
½ teaspoon ground cloves
½ teaspoon ground cardamom
¼ teaspoon black pepper
1 cup granulated sugar
1 cup butter, softened
¼ cup dark molasses
1 egg
Powdered sugar

1. Combine flour, baking powder, cinnamon, ginger, baking soda, salt, cloves, cardamom and pepper in large bowl.

2. Beat granulated sugar and butter in large bowl with electric mixer at medium speed until light and fluffy. Beat in molasses and egg. Gradually add flour mixture. Beat at low speed until dough forms. Shape dough into disc; wrap in plastic wrap and refrigerate until firm, 30 minutes or up to 3 days.

3. Preheat oven to 350°F. Grease cookie sheets. Roll dough into 1-inch balls. Place 2 inches apart on prepared cookie sheets.

4. Bake 12 to 14 minutes or until golden brown. Transfer cookies to wire racks; dust with sifted powdered sugar. Cool completely. Store tightly covered at room temperature or freeze up to 3 months.

Makes about 5 dozen cookies

Pfeffernüesse

Lemon Coconut Pixies

1 cup sugar
¹/₄ cup (¹/₂ stick) butter or margarine, softened
2 eggs
1¹/₂ teaspoons freshly grated lemon peel
1¹/₂ cups all-purpose flour
2 teaspoons baking powder
¹/₄ teaspoon salt
1 cup MOUNDS™ Sweetened Coconut Flakes
Powdered sugar

1. Heat oven to 300°F.

2. Beat sugar, butter, eggs and lemon peel in large bowl until well blended. Stir together flour, baking powder and salt; gradually add to lemon mixture, beating until blended. Stir in coconut. Cover; refrigerate dough about 1 hour or until firm enough to handle. Shape into 1-inch balls; roll in powdered sugar. Place 2 inches apart on ungreased cookie sheet.

3. Bake 15 to 18 minutes or until edges are set. Immediately remove from cookie sheet to wire rack. Cool completely. Store in tightly covered container in cool, dry place.   *Makes about 4 dozen cookies*

Lemon Coconut Pixies

Hershey's Soft & Chewy Cookies

1 cup (2 sticks) butter (no substitutes)
³/₄ cup packed light brown sugar
¹/₂ cup granulated sugar
¹/₄ cup light corn syrup
1 egg
2 teaspoons vanilla extract
2¹/₂ cups all-purpose flour
1 teaspoon baking soda
¹/₄ teaspoon salt
1 package (10 to 12 ounces) HERSHEY'S Chips or
   Baking Bits (any flavor)

1. *Heat oven to 350°F.*

2. *Beat butter, brown sugar and granulated sugar in large bowl until fluffy. Add corn syrup, egg and vanilla; beat well. Stir together flour, baking soda and salt; gradually add to butter mixture, beating until well blended. Stir in chips or bits. Drop by rounded teaspoons onto ungreased cookie sheet.*

3. *Bake 8 to 10 minutes or until lightly browned and almost set. Cool slightly; remove from cookie sheet to wire rack. Cool completely. Cookies will be softer the second day.*

Makes about 3¹/₂ dozen cookies

Chocolate Chocolate Cookies: *Decrease flour to 2¹/₄ cups and add ¹/₄ cup HERSHEY'S Cocoa or HERSHEY'S Dutch Processed Cocoa.*

Hershey's Soft & Chewy Cookies

Oatmeal Hermits

3 cups QUAKER® Oats (quick or old fashioned,
uncooked)
1 cup all-purpose flour
1 cup (2 sticks) butter or margarine, melted
1 cup firmly packed brown sugar
1 cup raisins
$^1/_2$ cup chopped nuts
1 egg
$^1/_4$ cup milk
1 teaspoon ground cinnamon
1 teaspoon vanilla
$^1/_2$ teaspoon baking soda
$^1/_2$ teaspoon salt (optional)
$^1/_4$ teaspoon ground nutmeg

Heat oven to 375°F. In large bowl, combine all ingredients; mix well.
Drop by rounded tablespoonfuls onto ungreased cookie sheets. Bake
8 to 10 minutes. Cool 1 minute on cookie sheets; remove to wire
cooling racks.   *Makes about 3 dozen*

For Bar Cookies: Press dough into ungreased 15×10-inch jelly-roll
pan. Bake about 17 minutes or until golden brown. Cool completely;
cut into bars.

Tip: The best cookie sheets to use are those with
little or no sides. They allow the heat to
circulate easily during baking and promote
even browning.

The publisher would like to thank the companies and organizations listed below for the use of their recipes and photographs in this publication.

Bob Evans®

Cherry Marketing Institute

Del Monte Corporation

Dole Food Company, Inc.

The Golden Grain Company®

Grandma's® is a registered trademark of Mott's, LLP

Hershey Foods Corporation

MASTERFOODS USA

National Honey Board

Nestlé USA

Northwest Cherry Growers

The Quaker® Oatmeal Kitchens

Reckitt Benckiser Inc.

Sargento® Foods Inc.

StarKist Seafood Company

The Sugar Association, Inc.

Reprinted with permission of Sunkist Growers, Inc.

Unilever Bestfoods North America

VOLUME MEASUREMENTS (dry)

1/8 teaspoon = 0.5 mL
1/4 teaspoon = 1 mL
1/2 teaspoon = 2 mL
3/4 teaspoon = 4 mL
1 teaspoon = 5 mL
1 tablespoon = 15 mL
2 tablespoons = 30 mL
1/4 cup = 60 mL
1/3 cup = 75 mL
1/2 cup = 125 mL
2/3 cup = 150 mL
3/4 cup = 175 mL
1 cup = 250 mL
2 cups = 1 pint = 500 mL
3 cups = 750 mL
4 cups = 1 quart = 1 L

VOLUME MEASUREMENTS (fluid)

1 fluid ounce (2 tablespoons) = 30 mL
4 fluid ounces (1/2 cup) = 125 mL
8 fluid ounces (1 cup) = 250 mL
12 fluid ounces (1 1/2 cups) = 375 mL
16 fluid ounces (2 cups) = 500 mL

WEIGHTS (mass)

1/2 ounce = 15 g
1 ounce = 30 g
3 ounces = 90 g
4 ounces = 120 g
8 ounces = 225 g
10 ounces = 285 g
12 ounces = 360 g
16 ounces = 1 pound = 450 g

DIMENSIONS

1/16 inch = 2 mm
1/8 inch = 3 mm
1/4 inch = 6 mm
1/2 inch = 1.5 cm
3/4 inch = 2 cm
1 inch = 2.5 cm

OVEN TEMPERATURES

250°F = 120°C
275°F = 140°C
300°F = 150°C
325°F = 160°C
350°F = 180°C
375°F = 190°C
400°F = 200°C
425°F = 220°C
450°F = 230°C

BAKING PAN SIZES

Utensil	Size in Inches/Quarts	Metric Volume	Size in Centimeters
Baking or	8×8×2	2 L	20×20×5
Cake Pan	9×9×2	2.5 L	23×23×5
(square or	12×8×2	3 L	30×20×5
rectangular)	13×9×2	3.5 L	33×23×5
Loaf Pan	8×4×3	1.5 L	20×10×7
	9×5×3	2 L	23×13×7
Round Layer	8×1½	1.2 L	20×4
Cake Pan	9×1½	1.5 L	23×4
Pie Plate	8×1¼	750 mL	20×3
	9×1¼	1 L	23×3
Baking Dish	1 quart	1 L	—
or Casserole	1½ quart	1.5 L	—
	2 quart	2 L	—